Cooperative Learning &
Literature

Stefanie McKoy

Kagan

Kagan Publishing
981 Calle Amanecer
San Clemente, CA 92673
1 (800) 933-2667
www.KaganOnline.com

ISBN: 978-1-933445-22-9

Cooperative Learning & Literature

~ Featured Books ~

Books

Cooperative Learning & Literature
Table of Contents

Amber Brown Is Not a Crayon
by Paula Danziger

Table of Activities

Because of Winn-Dixie
by Kate DiCamillo

The Boxcar Children
by Gertrude Chandler Warner

Table of Activities continued

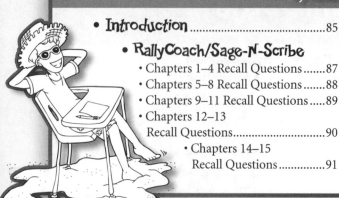

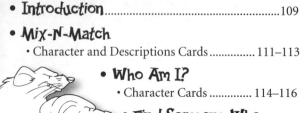
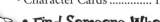

Cooperative Learning & Literature
Kagan Publishing • (800) 933-2667 • www.KaganOnline.com

Table of Activities continued

Henry and Ribsy
by Beverly Cleary

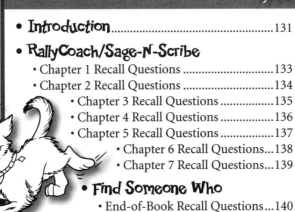

Little House in the Big Woods
by Laura Ingalls Wilder

Table of Activities continued

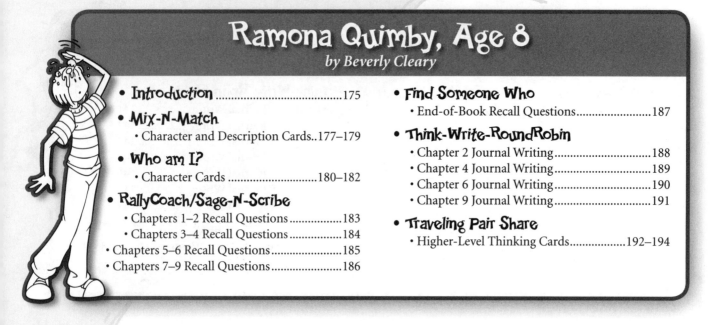

Table of Activities continued

Stuart Little
by E. B. White

The Whipping Boy
by Sid Fleischman

Activities for Any Literature Selection

Introduction

Dear Educators,

First, I want to thank you for picking up this resource to use with your class. I have worked very hard to bring these great examples of children's literature to life through classroom activities.

This project began a few years ago as I began to use Kagan Structures to engage my students. I began to use the structures to challenge students with literature-based questions that went beyond solo student work. I am very passionate about getting students motivated to read and love doing it, but students will still be expected to answer questions on a test.

I found myself creating structure-based activities for every book my students read and thought I should share this work with other teachers. I tried to pick literature that was popular in wide circles, won national awards, and were my students' favorites. In large part, my students for the past 2 years have played a big part in helping me create this book. They assisted me in choosing the stories to include and acting as mini-editors alongside me as we fine-tuned the questions.

The activities are based on nine Kagan Structures: Fan-N-Pick, Find Someone Who, Mix-N-Match, Traveling Pair Share, RallyCoach, Sage-N-Scribe, Showdown, Think-Write-RoundRobin and Who Am I?. Included are structures for pair work, team work, and whole-class interactions. Each structure is highly interactive and encourages teamwork among students about literature. Students love collaborating over the reading, and the process is excellent for developing understanding, deepening students' thinking, and improving their literacy skills.

This book is one of the first I have written by myself and it makes me truly miss my co-author Melissa Agnew. Her organization and attention to details make her a great partner, but I understand her decision to focus on her new little bundle of joy at home. However, her guidance is still appreciated as she was my sounding board through this project. I also need to thank the students who helped me endlessly check my activities for correct answers and grammar! They loved acting as mini-editors and suggesting books for me to include.

My fellow teachers at Branson Elementary West, as well as my principal, have been a huge support. They have tried out activities with their own students and answered any questions I might have about the skills I targeted. Of course, I could not have completed this project without the love and support of my family. Their encouragement has kept me going throughout this entire project.

A special thank you and appreciation goes to my students who helped write many of the story summaries. They brought insight and wisdom from a child's perspective. They are Kimi Steele, Kammi Bicek, Irielle McConnell, Maddie Pardeck, Kyla French, and Angelina Dillon.

Finally, I must thank those at Kagan for working with me on another project and trusting me with this responsibility. Appreciation goes to Miguel Kagan for his guidance and review of my manuscript; Alex Core for making the book come alive with his design and cover color; Becky Herrington for managing the publication; Erin Kant for illustrations; and Ginny Harvey for copy editing.

Happy Teaching!

Stefanie McKoy

Stefanie McKoy
Educator

About the Author

Stefanie McKoy graduated from Missouri State University in Springfield, Missouri, with a Bachelor of Arts degree in Elementary Education and holds a Master of Arts degree in Educational Technology Leadership from the University of Arkansas in Fayetteville, Arkansas. She is currently certified in both Early Childhood and Elementary Education in addition to her eMINTS certification. Stefanie teaches third grade at Branson School District. She has served on the school's communication arts committee and was coordinator for the after-school tutoring program serving four grade levels and more than 100 students. This past year, she has been co-teaching with the special education department serving eight learning disabled students in her regular education classroom. Stefanie resides in Ozark, Missouri, with her husband and their young son. She enjoys reading, building websites, and drinking a variety of gourmet coffees.

Cooperative Learning & Literature
Kagan Publishing • (800) 933-2667 • www.KaganOnline.com

Structures

Ramona Quimby

Howie Kemp

Fan-N-Pick

Teammates rotate roles as they ask, answer, paraphrase and praise, or coach each other.

Setup: Each team receives a set of question or problem cards.

1 Student #1 Fans Cards
Student #1 holds the question cards in a fan and says, "*Pick a card, any card!*"

2 Student #2 Picks a Card
Student #2 picks a card, reads the question aloud, to the team, holds the card up so student #3 can see the question for five seconds and then lays the card down. (For cards that have answers on thc back, student #2 passes the card to student #4 to check for correctness.)

3 Student #3 Answers
Student #3 answers the question.

4 Student #4 Responds
Student #4 responds to the answer.
• For right or wrong answers: Student #4 checks the answer and then either praises or tutors the student who answered. "*That's correct! You're a true genius.*" or "*I don't think that's correct; let's solve it again together.*"

• For higher-level thinking questions that have no right or wrong answer: Student #4 does not check for correctness, but praises the thinking that went into the answer and/or paraphrases. "*You gave three plausible changes that Henry had to make in his routine in order to go fishing. I like the way you approached the question.*"

5 Rotate Roles
Teammates rotate roles, one person clockwise for each new round.

Cooperative Learning & Literature
Kagan Publishing • (800) 933-2667 • www.KaganOnline.com

~Fan-N-Pick Activities~

Find Someone Who

Students are excited, circulating through the classroom, forming and reforming pairs, trying to "find someone who" knows an answer; and then they become "someone who knows."

Setup: The teacher prepares a worksheet or questions for students.

1 Students Mix
With worksheets in one hand and the other hand raised, students circulate through the room until they find a partner. *"Mix in the room and pair up with a student with a hand up. Put your hands down, and each asks each other one question from your sheet. If your partner knows an answer, write the answer in your own words, and then have your partner sign your sheet to show agreement."*

2 Partner A Asks a Question
In pairs, Partner A asks a question from the worksheet; Partner B answers. Partner A records the answer on his or her own worksheet.

3 Partner B Checks
Partner B checks the answer and initials it, indicating agreement.

4 Partner B Asks a Question
Partner B now asks a question; Partner A responds. Partner B records the answer on his or her own worksheet.

5 Partner A Checks
Partner A checks the answer and initials indicating agreement.

6 Partners Depart
Partners shake hands, part, and raise a hand again as they search for a new partner.

7 Continue Finding Someone Who
Students continue mixing and pairing until their worksheets are complete.

8 Students Sit
When their worksheets are completed, students sit down; seated students may be approached by others as a resource. Alternatively, finished students may stand along a wall or on the outside perimeter of the room.

9 Teams Compare Answers
When all students are done, or the teacher calls time, students return to their teams to compare answers; in the case of disagreement or uncertainty, they can consult a neighbor team or raise four hands to ask a team question. *"Please return to your team and then RoundRobin read the question and share the answer. If you have different answers, work it out in your team. If you can't agree, get help from a nearby team, or raise four hands to ask a team question."*

~ Find Someone Who Activities ~

The Preacher

Opal's father, Opal describes him as a turtle who hides in his shell, thinks about or is preaching at all times, misses Opal's mother.

Mix-N-Match

Students mix, repeatedly quizzing new partners and trading cards. Afterwards, they rush to find a partner with the card that matches theirs.

Setup: The teacher provides or students create pairs of matching cards. One card may have a character's name and the other a description of that character.

1 Students Mix and Pair
With a card in one hand and the other hand raised, each student mixes around the room, looking for a partner with a raised hand. When they pair up, they give each other a high five. "*Pair up with another student with a raised hand. Give each other a high five and then lower your hands.*"

2 Partner A Asks a Question
In the pair, Partner A asks Partner B a question from his or her card. For example Partner A's card says, The Preacher, "*How would you describe this character?*"

3 Partner B Answers
Partner B answers Partner A's question. "*He is Opal's father and he is preaching at all times.*"

4 Partner A Praises or Coaches
If Partner B answers correctly, Partner A provides praise. "*Right! You are great at remembering the story!*" If Partner B answers incorrectly, Partner A provides the correct answer and coaches or tutors Partner B. "*Not quite! Let's look back in the pages to get clarity.*"

5 Switch Roles
Partners switch roles. Partner B now asks the question and offers praise or coaching.

6 Partners Trade Cards
Before departing and looking for new partners, partners trade cards.

7 Continue Quizzing and Trading
Partners split up and continue quizzing and getting quizzed by new partners. When done, they trade cards again and find a new partner.

8 Teacher Calls "Freeze"
After a sufficient time of quizzing and trading cards, the teacher calls "*Freeze.*" Students freeze, hide their cards, and think of their match.

9 Find Match
The teacher calls "*Match.*" Students search for a classmate with the matching card. When they find each other, they move to the outside of the classroom and stand shoulder to shoulder. This way, students still searching for a match can find each other more easily.

10 Teacher Checks Answer
The teacher selects a pair to begin. The pair shares their answer by stating what they have on their own cards. Alternatively, the teacher has students hold up their cards and does a quick visual answer check.

Mix-N-Match Activities

Traveling Pair Share

Students travel around the classroom and pair up with classmates to ask and answer questions.

Setup: Give each student a question card.

1 Students Pair Up
Students stand up, put a hand up, and high five to pair up with a classmate.

2 Partner Reads Question
One partner reads a question from the selected question card. For example, *"What is the significance of Opal bathing and grooming Winn-Dixie after adopting him?"*

3 Other Partner Answers
The other partner answers the question.

4 Partners Switch Roles
The student who answered the question now asks the question on his or her question card and his or her partner responds. For example, *"If Winn-Dixie's Grocery store manager had caught Winn-Dixie, how might the story have changed?"*

5 Continue Pairing
After both partners respond, they give each other a high five, put a hand up, and then travel around the classroom to find a new partner. They continue asking and responding to the questions on their question cards.

Cooperative Learning & Literature
Kagan Publishing • (800) 933-2667 • www.KaganOnline.com

∼ Traveling Pair Share Activities ∼

RallyCoach

In pairs, students take turns each solving a problem while the other coaches.

Setup: The teacher prepares a set of problems. Each pair receives only one pencil or pen and one problem worksheet or a piece of paper to answer the problems.

1 Partner A Solves
In shoulder partners, Partner A solves the first problem, explaining the thinking to his or her partner.

2 Partner B Coaches and Praises
Partner B acts as the coach. Partner B watches, listens, and checks. If Partner A gets an incorrect answer or needs help, Partner B coaches. If Partner A solves the problem correctly, Partner B praises.

3 Partner B Solves
Students switch roles and Partner B now solves the next problem, talking it out.

4 Partner A Coaches and Praises
Partner A now acts as the coach: watching, listening, checking, coaching and praising.

5 Continue Solving
The process is repeated for each new problem.

Cooperative Learning & Literature
Kagan Publishing • (800) 933-2667 • www.KaganOnline.com

～ RallyCoach Activities ～

Sage-N-Scribe

In pairs, students solve problems, taking turns playing the roles of the Sage and the Scribe.

Setup: In pairs, Student A is the Sage; Student B is the Scribe. Each pair is given a set of problems to solve. Partners share one problem worksheet and one pencil or pen.

1 Sage Instructs Scribe
The Sage orally instructs the Scribe how to perform a task or solve a problem. For example, the Sage's instructions to the Scribe for answering a recall question about *Henry and Ribsy* might sound like this: "*Circle b, Chasing the Grumbies' cat. Remember Ribsy loved chasing all moving critters.*"

2 Scribe Writes a Solution, Tutors if Necessary
The Scribe solves the problem in writing according to the Sage's step-by-step oral instructions. If the Sage gives incorrect instructions, the Scribe tutors the Sage. "*I think we missed it! Let's reread that part of the story.*"

3 Scribe Praises Sage
After completion of the problem, the Scribe praises the Sage. "*You aced that one!*"

4 Partners Switch Roles
Students switch roles for the next problem or task.

Cooperative Learning & Literature
Kagan Publishing • (800) 933-2667 • www.KaganOnline.com

～ Sage-N-Scribe Activities ～

Showdown

Students independently answer a question, and then have a "Showdown" displaying their answers to teammates.

Setup: The teacher prepares questions or problems. Questions may be provided to each team as question cards that they stack face down in the center of the table. Each student has a slate or a response board and a writing utensil.

1 Teacher Selects a Showdown Captain
The teacher selects one student on each team to be the Showdown Captain for the first round. "*Student #4 is the first Showdown Captain. Rotate the role clockwise after each question.*"

2 Showdown Captain Reads a Question
The Showdown Captain reads the first question. If using question cards, the Showdown Captain draws the top card, reads the question, shows it to the team, and provides think time. "*Think about your answer, then write it down.*"

3 Students Answer Independently
Working alone, all students write their answers and keep their answers hidden from teammates.

4 Teammates Signal When Done
When finished, teammates signal they're ready by turning over their response boards, putting down their markers, or giving a hand signal.

5 Showdown Captain Calls "Showdown"
The Showdown Captain calls "*Showdown!*"

6 Teams Show Answers
Teammates simultaneously show their answers and RoundRobin state them in turn.

7 Teams Check for Accuracy
The Showdown Captain leads the team in checking for accuracy. "*Great. We all got the same answer.*"

8 Celebrate or Coach
If all the teammates have the correct answer, the Showdown Captain is Team Cheerleader. If a teammate has an incorrect answer, teammates coach the student or students with the incorrect answer, and then celebrate.

9 Rotate Captain Role
The person on the left of the Showdown Captain becomes the Showdown Captain for the next round.

Cooperative Learning & Literature
Kagan Publishing • (800) 933-2667 • www.KaganOnline.com

Showdown Activities

✦ **Amber Brown is Not a Crayon**
  • End-of-Book Recall Questions 38–39

✦ **Because of Winn-Dixie**
  • End-of-Book Recall Questions 57–58

✦ **Little House in the Big Woods**
  • End-of-Book Recall Questions 165–166

✦ **Stuart Little**
  • End-of-Book Recall Questions 223–224

Think-Write-RoundRobin

*Students take turns sharing
their writing with teammates.*

Setup: The teacher prepares a set of questions or a writing assignment. Each teammate receives a pen or pencil and a piece of paper to record his or her response or responses.

1 Teacher Assigns a Task
Teacher presents a question or assigns a writing (or drawing) task.

2 Teacher Provides Think Time
Teacher provides students with Think Time to think of their responses.

3 Students Write
Students write (or draw) their responses.

4 Students Share
Students share their writing with their teammates, using RoundRobin, each sharing in turn what they wrote.

Note:
In this book, Think-Write-RoundRobin is used to respond to a journal prompt. For these activities, the Think-Write-RoundRobin is preceded by a RoundRobin for teammates to share their ideas about the question before they write. In the second RoundRobin, teammates share their journal writing with teammates.

Cooperative Learning & Literature
Kagan Publishing • (800) 933-2667 • www.KaganOnline.com

~Think-Write-RoundRobin Activities~

Who Am I?

Students pair up with classmates to ask questions, attempting to discover their secret identity.

Setup: The teacher or students make cards. One card is carefully placed on each student's back so students do not see who or what they are.

1 Students Pair Up
Students stand up and raise a hand until they find a partner. The pair gives a high five and then lowers their hands. *"Find a classmate with a hand up. Give each other a high five and then lower your hands."*

2 Partner A Asks Three Questions
Partner A turns around to show Partner B the card on his or her back. Partner A asks Partner B three yes-or-no questions to discover the secret identity. Questions might be: *"(1) Am I a person? (2) Am I male? (3) Am I a child?"* Partner B answers *"yes"* or *"no"* to each question.

3 Partner B Asks Three Questions
Reverse roles. Partner B now asks three questions and Partner A answers.

4 Students Form New Partners and Continue
Partners shake hands, thank each other, and raise their hands to find a new partner.

Note:
When it's their turn, students may make one guess at their identity with each partner. If they are wrong, they keep playing. If they are right, they move their identity card to their front, and become a helper, whispering clues to classmates.

For example, a clue about Tick from *Gregor the Overlander* might be: *"You sacrificed yourself to save Temp."* A clue about Temp from *Gregor the Overlander* might be: *"Tick sacrificed herself to save you."*

Cooperative Learning & Literature
Kagan Publishing • (800) 933-2667 • www.KaganOnline.com

Who Am I? Activities

Literature Activities

Amber Brown Is Not a Crayon

By Paula Danziger

This story is about two kids who have been best friends since preschool, named Amber Brown and Justin Daniels. Amber learns that Justin is moving to Alabama with his family and they begin fighting. Amber thinks this is the worst year of her life and she has to think about making new friends. Will they be able to work it out before it is too late? With the help of her mother, Amber discovers that good friends never have to lose one another.

Reading Level

Lexile Level: 720
Guided Reading Level: N
DRA Level: 30
Accelerated Reader: 3.7

Amber Brown Is Not a Crayon

～ Cooperative Learning Activities ～

Recall Questions
Amber Brown Is Not a Crayon • Chapters 1–3

❏ **RallyCoach Directions:** Take turns answering each question as your partner coaches. Explain your thinking to your coach.

❏ **Sage-N-Scribe Directions:** The Sage describes what he or she knows about the question so the Scribe can answer the question. The Sage and Scribe switch roles for each question.

Amber Brown Is Not a Crayon

Name _____

1. In what grade is Amber Brown?
 a. 1st grade
 b. 2nd grade
 c. 3rd grade
 d. 4th grade

2. How does Mr. Cohen let the students know it is time to switch activities?
 a. claps his hands three times
 b. flicks the lights off
 c. raises his hands
 d. rings a bell on his desk

3. Which of the following is not an example of how Justin and Amber make a great team?
 a. They whisper words to each other in reading groups.
 b. Amber's handwriting is better and Justin is very neat about pasting things.
 c. They learn things at about the same time.
 d. They are able to finish each other's sentences.

4. What did Justin's fortune cookie say?
 a. Soon you will be going on a new journey and beginning a new life.
 b. Experience is the best teacher.
 c. Actions speak louder than words.
 d. Something you lost will soon turn up.

5. How did Amber try to persuade Mrs. Bradley not to buy the house?
 a. She told her ghosts are in the attic.
 b. She told her the house is built on a cemetery.
 c. She told her alligators are in the toilet.
 d. She told her lions live in the closets.

Amber Brown Is Not a Crayon

Name _____

1. What word best describes Amber Brown?
 a. messy
 b. tidy
 c. clean
 d. average

2. Where was the class preparing to fly to in order to learn?
 a. Australia
 b. the Natural Arts Museum
 c. Canada
 d. China

3. Why was Justin's father in Alabama?
 a. His parents just got divorced.
 b. His dad was stationed there with the army.
 c. His dad got a new job.
 d. His parents were planning to open a store.

4. What do Justin and Amber eat for a snack when they get home?
 a. peanut butter sandwiches
 b. Oreo® cookies
 c. pretzels
 d. cheese crackers

5. What wallpaper did Justin and Amber want for the Danielses' kitchen?
 a. baseball player
 b. bowls of fruit
 c. flowers
 d. footballs

Recall Questions
Amber Brown Is Not a Crayon • Chapters 4–6

❑ **RallyCoach Directions:** Take turns answering each question as your partner coaches. Explain your thinking to your coach.

❑ **Sage-N-Scribe Directions:** The Sage describes what he or she knows about the question so the Scribe can answer the question. The Sage and Scribe switch roles for each question.

Amber Brown Is Not a Crayon

Name _____

1. **What book does Amber plan on reading for her project?**
   a. *Hatchet*
   b. *The Lion, the Witch, and the Wardrobe*
   c. *Mr. Popper's Penguins*
   d. *Charlotte's Web*

2. **What did Justin and Amber see when they finished hopping home?**
   a. a dog that got out through the fence
   b. a moving van outside Justin's house
   c. a "Sold" sticker on the For Sale sign
   d. Justin's mom crying about moving

3. **What did Amber eat while working on her China project?**
   a. peanut butter and M&M's® sandwich
   b. egg rolls and fried rice
   c. Oreo cookies and milk
   d. Chinese noodles

4. **How did Amber and Justin try to persuade Mr. Daniels not to take the new job?**
   a. promised to get all A's on their report card
   b. keep their rooms clean and make their beds
   c. give him part of Amber's allowance
   d. not ask for any new toys

5. **What was Mr. Cohen's class working on when Justin returned to class?**
   a. cause and effect
   b. fractions
   c. multiplication
   d. cursive handwriting

Amber Brown Is Not a Crayon

Name _____

1. **Why was Justin hopping on the way home from school?**
   a. He needed to practice for basketball.
   b. He was being a kangaroo.
   c. He wanted to be the best at leap frog.
   d. He didn't want to step on any cracks.

2. **Why did Justin miss three days of school?**
   a. He had the flu and was too sick for school.
   b. He flew to see Mr. Daniels and to look for a new house.
   c. He was visiting his grandparents.
   d. He had already moved to Alabama.

3. **Where is Amber's father?**
   a. China
   b. France
   c. England
   d. Alabama

4. **What was the one good thought Amber was able to think about regarding Justin moving?**
   a. They could write letters to each other.
   b. Amber could talk on the phone every night.
   c. Amber would be able to find a new friend.
   d. Amber can store some of her stuff in Justin's desk.

5. **Which of the following is a difference between Justin's old school and new school?**
   a. Both have a lot of students.
   b. His old school has air-conditioning.
   c. His new school has a cafeteria.
   d. Both schools are new.

Cooperative Learning & Literature
Kagan Publishing • (800) 933-2667 • www.KaganOnline.com

Recall Questions
Amber Brown Is Not a Crayon • Chapters 7–9

❏ **RallyCoach Directions:** Take turns answering each question as your partner coaches. Explain your thinking to your coach.

❏ **Sage-N-Scribe Directions:** The Sage describes what he or she knows about the question so the Scribe can answer the question. The Sage and Scribe switch roles for each question.

Amber Brown Is Not a Crayon

Name _____

1. Which word best describes the Danielses' house during the move?
   a. neat and orderly
   b. a maze of boxes
   c. a natural disaster
   d. piles of garbage

2. Why does Amber not want to be best friends with Hannah Burton?
   a. Hannah is too busy.
   b. Amber wants a boy as a best friend.
   c. Hannah is too neat and wants to look good.
   d. Amber doesn't like to wear dresses.

3. What had Amber drawn on Justin's picture?
   a. elephant ears
   b. chicken pox
   c. a mustache
   d. a clown hat

4. What did Amber think Mr. Cohen said as she went into the hallway with Justin?
   a. *"Finally!"*
   b. *"About time!"*
   c. *"At last!"*
   d. *"Friends!"*

Amber Brown Is Not a Crayon

Name _____

1. Why did Amber say she was never going to speak to Justin Daniels again?
   a. He was happy about moving to Alabama.
   b. He tossed out their school picture.
   c. He wouldn't give Amber his favorite football card.
   d. He threw away their chewing gum ball.

2. What food does Amber's mom offer her for comfort?
   a. double-fudge brownie mix, unbaked
   b. raw white chocolate chip cookie dough
   c. strawberry ice cream with whipped cream
   d. fudge popsicle with a banana-cream center

3. How did Mr. Cohen's class say goodbye to Justin?
   a. made him an extra large card
   b. created a class scrapbook
   c. had a pizza party
   d. wrote Justin a story about his class

4. What present did Justin give Amber?
   a. his pilot wings
   b. the chewing gum ball
   c. an Alabama sweatshirt
   d. his football card collection

Recall Questions
Amber Brown Is Not a Crayon • End-of-Book

Directions: Copy one set of cards for each team. Cut out each card along the dotted line. Give each team a set of cards to play Fan-N-Pick or Showdown.

① Amber Brown Is Not a Crayon

What did the boys do when they received peanuts during the pretend flight?

Fan-N-Pick/Showdown

② Amber Brown Is Not a Crayon

What was the true reason Amber was mad at Justin?

Fan-N-Pick/Showdown

③ Amber Brown Is Not a Crayon

What did Mr. Cohen's class do as a way to goodbye to Justin?

Fan-N-Pick/Showdown

④ Amber Brown Is Not a Crayon

Where did Mr. Cohen take his class during their pretend flight?

Fan-N-Pick/Showdown

⑤ Amber Brown Is Not a Crayon

What did Amber tell Mrs. Bradley about the Danielses' house?

Fan-N-Pick/Showdown

⑥ Amber Brown Is Not a Crayon

Why was Justin's father in Alabama?

Fan-N-Pick/Showdown

⑦ Amber Brown Is Not a Crayon

What present did Justin give Amber before leaving?

Fan-N-Pick/Showdown

⑧ Amber Brown Is Not a Crayon

What grade did Mr. Cohen teach?

Fan-N-Pick/Showdown

Cooperative Learning & Literature
Kagan Publishing • (800) 933-2667 • www.KaganOnline.com

Recall Questions
Amber Brown Is Not a Crayon • End-of-Book

Directions: Copy one set of cards for each team. Cut out each card along the dotted line. Give each team a set of cards to play Fan-N-Pick or Showdown.

9 Amber Brown Is Not a Crayon Why did Amber and Justin work on their China scrapbook together? *Fan-N-Pick/Showdown*	**10** Amber Brown Is Not a Crayon What was Justin wearing when he told the class about his trip? *Fan-N-Pick/Showdown*
11 Amber Brown Is Not a Crayon What important item does Amber need from her desk in order to go on the trip? *Fan-N-Pick/Showdown*	**12** Amber Brown Is Not a Crayon Why doesn't Amber want to be a flight attendant when it is her turn to get picked? *Fan-N-Pick/Showdown*
13 Amber Brown Is Not a Crayon What does Hannah always complain about? *Fan-N-Pick/Showdown*	**14** Amber Brown Is Not a Crayon What tool does Hanna say Amber combs her hair with? *Fan-N-Pick/Showdown*
15 Amber Brown Is Not a Crayon What nickname does Justin have for his little brother? *Fan-N-Pick/Showdown*	**16** Amber Brown Is Not a Crayon What eating utensil is Amber not very good with? *Fan-N-Pick/Showdown*

Journal Writing
Amber Brown Is Not a Crayon • End-of-Book

Directions: Think about the Journal Question, and then write your own response. When done, RoundRobin share your writing with your teammates. Use the space at the bottom to record ideas your teammates share.

Journal Question
What lesson did the author want you to learn after reading
Amber Brown Is Not a Crayon? Support your answer using details from the story.

Journal Response _____

_____

_____

_____

_____

_____

_____

_____

_____

_____

_____

_____

_____

Ideas Teammates Shared

Cooperative Learning and Literature
Kagan Publishing • (800) 933-2667 • www.KaganOnline.com

Higher-Level Thinking Cards
Amber Brown Is Not a Crayon

Directions: Copy enough cards so that each student receives a Question Card. Have students stand up, pair up, and do Traveling Pair Share to respond to each other's questions. Students trade cards and find a new partner to share.

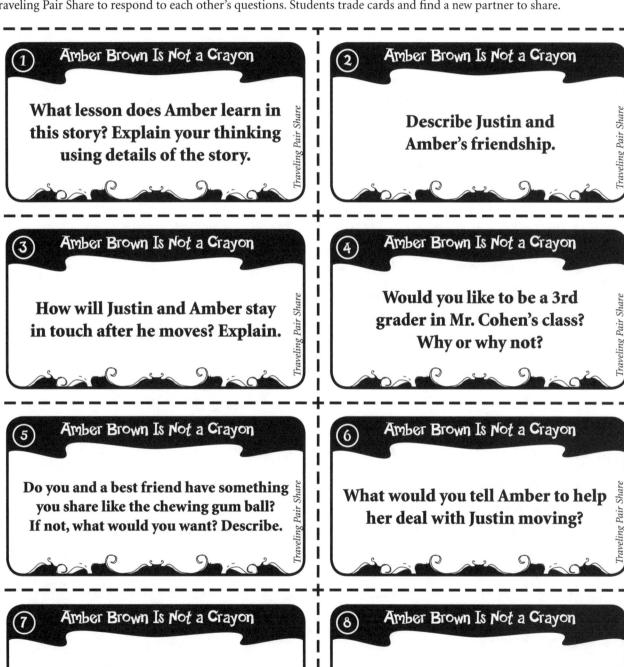

1 Amber Brown Is Not a Crayon

What lesson does Amber learn in this story? Explain your thinking using details of the story.

Traveling Pair Share

2 Amber Brown Is Not a Crayon

Describe Justin and Amber's friendship.

Traveling Pair Share

3 Amber Brown Is Not a Crayon

How will Justin and Amber stay in touch after he moves? Explain.

Traveling Pair Share

4 Amber Brown Is Not a Crayon

Would you like to be a 3rd grader in Mr. Cohen's class? Why or why not?

Traveling Pair Share

5 Amber Brown Is Not a Crayon

Do you and a best friend have something you share like the chewing gum ball? If not, what would you want? Describe.

Traveling Pair Share

6 Amber Brown Is Not a Crayon

What would you tell Amber to help her deal with Justin moving?

Traveling Pair Share

7 Amber Brown Is Not a Crayon

What qualities make a best friend? Explain.

Traveling Pair Share

8 Amber Brown Is Not a Crayon

Have you ever had a friend who had to move away? How did you feel?

Traveling Pair Share

Higher-Level Thinking Cards
Amber Brown Is Not a Crayon

Directions: Copy enough cards so that each student receives a Question Card. Have students stand up, pair up, and do Traveling Pair Share to respond to each other's questions. Students trade cards and find a new partner to share.

---

9 Amber Brown Is Not a Crayon

Amber says she is never going to speak to Justin again. Is this a good or bad way to deal with her anger? Explain.

Traveling Pair Share

---

10 Amber Brown Is Not a Crayon

What do you think Justin and Amber will do during their summer visit? Describe.

Traveling Pair Share

---

11 Amber Brown Is Not a Crayon

What are the differences between Amber's school and your school? What is the same? Explain.

Traveling Pair Share

---

12 Amber Brown Is Not a Crayon

How does Justin feel about moving to Alabama? Explain.

Traveling Pair Share

---

13 Amber Brown Is Not a Crayon

Have you ever had to move? What was it like? Did you want to move?

Traveling Pair Share

---

14 Amber Brown Is Not a Crayon

If you could move anywhere, where would it be and why? Explain.

Traveling Pair Share

---

15 Amber Brown Is Not a Crayon

What will Amber do after Justin leaves? Describe.

Traveling Pair Share

---

16 Amber Brown Is Not a Crayon

What is the most important quality to have in a friend? Explain.

Traveling Pair Share

Cooperative Learning & Literature
Kagan Publishing • (800) 933-2667 • www.KaganOnline.com

Because of Winn-Dixie

By Kate DiCamillo

Opal finds a dog at the grocery store. Because the storeowner was going to call the pound, Opal claimed the dog was hers. She chose the name Winn-Dixie because they were at the Winn-Dixie grocery store and it was the first thing that came to mind. Opal takes Winn-Dixie everywhere, and more times than not, they get into some sort of mischief. One day after hearing the bear story from Miss Franny Block at the library, on their way home, Winn-Dixie chases a cat into Gloria Dump's yard and Opal meets Gloria Dump whom the Dewberry boys claim is a witch. More and more relationships and friendships develop, and Opal and Gloria decide to have a party. Opal invites many friends and not-so-good-friends, and when the party starts, thunder scares Winn-Dixie and he disappears. Will they find him? Opal makes many friends all due to the whims of Winn-Dixie. And even though there are many different types of people at the party, Winn-Dixie brings them together by learning to care for each other even with their differences.

Reading Level
Lexile Level: 610
Guided Reading Level: R
DRA Level: 40
Accelerated Reader: 3.9

Because of Winn-Dixie

～ Cooperative Learning Activities ～

Cooperative Learning & Literature
Kagan Publishing • (800) 933-2667 • www.KaganOnline.com

Character and Description Cards
Because of Winn-Dixie

Directions: Cut out each card along the dotted line. Matching cards are presented side by side in the book. Give each student one matching card to play Mix-N-Match.

Because of Winn-Dixie

How would you describe this character?

The Preacher

Mix-N-Match

Because of Winn-Dixie

Which character matches this description?

Opal's father, Opal describes him as a turtle who hides in his shell, thinks about or is preaching at all times, misses Opal's mother.

Mix-N-Match

Because of Winn-Dixie

How would you describe this character?

India Opal

Mix-N-Match

Because of Winn-Dixie

Which character matches this description?

The main character, lonely girl who goes on a journey of finding friends after moving to Naomi, Florida, accepts the differences in others.

Mix-N-Match

Because of Winn-Dixie

How would you describe this character?

Miss Franny Block

Mix-N-Match

Because of Winn-Dixie

Which character matches this description?

Town librarian who befriends Opal and Winn-Dixie, shares stories with Opal about her great-grandfather and bears.

Mix-N-Match

Because of Winn-Dixie

How would you describe this character?

Gloria Dump

Mix-N-Match

Because of Winn-Dixie

Which character matches this description?

Called a witch by the Dewberry boys; an older lady who has a mistake tree, has bad eyesight so she "sees" with her heart, and wise.

Mix-N-Match

Character and Description Cards
Because of Winn-Dixie

Directions: Cut out each card along the dotted line. Matching cards are presented side by side in the book. Give each student one matching card to play Mix-N-Match.

Because of Winn-Dixie *How would you describe this character?* **Sweetie Pie Thomas**	**Because of Winn-Dixie** *Which character matches this description?* **Young girl who wants a dog but her mom won't let her have one, turns 6 in September and invites Opal to her birthday party, making Opal feel welcome.**
Because of Winn-Dixie *How would you describe this character?* **Winn-Dixie**	**Because of Winn-Dixie** *Which character matches this description?* **The dog that helps Opal make friends in Naomi, loves peanut butter, smiles with all his teeth, has a pathological fear of thunderstorms.**
Because of Winn-Dixie *How would you describe this character?* **Otis**	**Because of Winn-Dixie** *Which character matches this description?* **Works at Gertrude's Pets, plays guitar, shy, spent time in jail.**
Because of Winn-Dixie *How would you describe this character?* **Dunlap and Stevie Dewberry**	**Because of Winn-Dixie** *Which character matches this description?* **Opal calls them the bald-headed babies; they are mean to Opal but Opal becomes friends with them at the end.**

Cooperative Learning & Literature
Kagan Publishing • (800) 933-2667 • www.KaganOnline.com

Character and Description Cards
Because of Winn-Dixie

Directions: Cut out each card along the dotted line. Matching cards are presented side by side in the book. Give each student one matching card to play Mix-N-Match.

Because of Winn-Dixie

How would you describe this character?
Amanda Wilkinson

Mix-N-Match

Because of Winn-Dixie

Which character matches this description?
Opal calls her pinched face until she learns her brother, Carson, drowned the year before, become unlikely friends in the end.

Mix-N-Match

Because of Winn-Dixie

How would you describe this character?
Mrs. Detweller

Mix-N-Match

Because of Winn-Dixie

Which character matches this description?
Lived in Friendly Corners Trailer Park, had a yappy Yorkie dog named Samuel.

Mix-N-Match

Because of Winn-Dixie

How would you describe this character?
Mr. Alfred

Mix-N-Match

Because of Winn-Dixie

Which character matches this description?
Friendly Corners Trailer Park manager. Did not like kids in the senior trailer park. Made Opal an "exception" because she was quiet.

Mix-N-Match

Because of Winn-Dixie

How would you describe this character?

Write in your own character.

Mix-N-Match

Because of Winn-Dixie

Which character matches this description?

Write in your own description.

Mix-N-Match

Character Cards
Because of Winn-Dixie

Directions: Copy the Character Cards for *Because of Winn-Dixie* by Kate DiCamillo, one per student. Cut each card along the dotted line and follow the directions for Who Am I?.

① Because of Winn-Dixie

The Preacher

Who Am I?

② Because of Winn-Dixie

India Opal

Who Am I?

③ Because of Winn-Dixie

Franny Block

Who Am I?

④ Because of Winn-Dixie

Gloria Dump

Who Am I?

Cooperative Learning & Literature
Kagan Publishing • (800) 933-2667 • www.KaganOnline.com

Character Cards
Because of Winn-Dixie

Directions: Copy the Character Cards for *Because of Winn-Dixie* by Kate DiCamillo, one per student. Cut each card along the dotted line and follow the directions for Who Am I?.

⑤ **Because of Winn-Dixie**

Sweetie Pie Thomas

Who Am I?

⑥ **Because of Winn-Dixie**

Winn-Dixie

Who Am I?

⑦ **Because of Winn-Dixie**

Otis

Who Am I?

⑧ **Because of Winn-Dixie**

Dunlap and Stevie Dewberry

Who Am I?

Character Cards
Because of Winn-Dixie

Directions: Copy the Character Cards for *Because of Winn-Dixie* by Kate DiCamillo, one per student. Cut each card along the dotted line and follow the directions for Who Am I?.

⑨ **Because of Winn-Dixie**

Amanda Wilkinson

Who Am I?

⑩ **Because of Winn-Dixie**

Mrs. Detweller

Who Am I?

⑪ **Because of Winn-Dixie**

Mr. Alfred

Who Am I?

⑫ **Because of Winn-Dixie**

Write in your own character.

Who Am I?

Cooperative Learning & Literature
Kagan Publishing • (800) 933-2667 • www.KaganOnline.com

Recall Questions
Because of Winn-Dixie • Chapters 1–2

Directions: Participate in Find Someone Who to answer the recall questions about *Because of Winn-Dixie*. Circle the correct answer provided by your partner and have your partner initial the answer.

1 When does this story take place?

a. summer
b. fall
c. winter
d. spring

_____
Initials

2 What amazing thing did Opal see when she saw the dog?

a. The dog bowed his head.
b. The dog smiled.
c. The dog sneezed.
d. The dog barked.

_____
Initials

3 What prevented the dog from being sent to the pound?

a. The store owner decided to keep him.
b. The pound was closed that day.
c. Opal told the manager it was her dog.
d. The preacher said they would take him home.

_____
Initials

4 What conclusion can you make about how Opal came up with the name Winn-Dixie?

a. It was the name of her favorite book.
b. She had heard it once before and really liked it.
c. The store's name was Winn-Dixie.
d. Opal's favorite toy was named Winn-Dixie.

_____
Initials

5 Who is telling the story?

a. an unknown author
b. Winn-Dixie
c. Opal
d. Opal's mother

_____
Initials

6 How did Opal describe Winn-Dixie?

a. as a brown carpet that was left out in the rain
b. as a lonely dog in need of a caregiver
c. shaggy rug with bald spots
d. wet wig with stringy hair

_____
Initials

7 What caused Opal and her dad to move to Naomi, Florida?

a. Preacher needed to forget his past.
b. Opal wanted to visit her grandparents.
c. Preacher got a job at the Naomi church.

_____
Initials

8 What reason did Opal give for calling her father Preacher?

a. That was his birth name.
b. She couldn't say his real name and just called him Preacher like everyone else.
c. He was always preaching or thinking about preaching.
d. He wore a name tag that said Preacher when in church.

_____
Initials

9 How did Winn-Dixie greet the Preacher?

a. barked and licked his hand
b. ran circles around his desk scattering papers
c. sniffed his shoes and then sneezed
d. laid his head in Preacher's lap

_____
Initials

Recall Questions
Because of Winn-Dixie • Chapters 3–7

Directions: Participate in Find Someone Who to answer the recall questions about *Because of Winn-Dixie*. Circle the correct answer provided by your partner and have your partner initial the answer.

1 What was the first step Opal did to clean up Winn-Dixie?

a. brushed him
b. bathed him
c. dried him
d. cut his nails

_____ Initials

2 What prevented Opal from brushing Winn-Dixie's teeth?

a. He growled.
b. He didn't like the toothpaste.
c. He kept sneezing.
d. Opal didn't have a toothbrush.

_____ Initials

3 What was one thing that Opal's mom disliked?

a. gardening
b. being a preacher's wife
c. running
d. her red hair

_____ Initials

4 To what animal did Opal compare the Preacher?

a. a rabbit
b. a turtle
c. a horse
d. a cat

_____ Initials

5 What was the effect of leaving Winn-Dixie in the trailer alone?

a. howled continuously
b. pulled the toilet paper off the roll
c. chewed on the Preacher's shoes
d. ate all the fresh fruit on the counter

_____ Initials

6 What was the cause of Winn-Dixie's distraction during church?

a. Opal wasn't sitting beside him.
b. Winn-Dixie joined in on the hymns.
c. A young boy dropped a ball.
d. A mouse ran across the floor.

_____ Initials

7 What did Miss Franny Block receive as a birthday present when she was younger?

a. a large box full of brand new books
b. an entire library full of books
c. a story about a bear and a library
d. an extra bedroom next to hers with her favorite books

_____ Initials

8 How did Miss Franny get rid of the bear?

a. called the local sheriff
b. pulled out a shotgun and fired a warning shot
c. threw a book at him
d. shouted at the top of her lungs

_____ Initials

9 What genre of story is *Because of Winn-Dixie*?

a. fantasy
b. historical fiction
c. fairy tale
d. realistic fiction

_____ Initials

Cooperative Learning & Literature
Kagan Publishing • (800) 933-2667 • www.KaganOnline.com

Recall Questions
Because of Winn-Dixie • Chapters 8–10

Directions: Participate in Find Someone Who to answer the recall questions about *Because of Winn-Dixie*. Circle the correct answer provided by your partner and have your partner initial the answer.

1 What prevented Winn-Dixie from entering Gertrude's Pets?

a. The owner was allergic to dogs.
b. A sign was posted that read: NO DOGS ALLOWED.
c. Opal didn't want Winn-Dixie to scare the other animals.
d. Winn-Dixie was afraid of the loud noise coming from inside.

Initials

2 What was Opal's solution to getting the fancy collar and leash?

a. asking her dad for a raise in her allowance
b. selling her used books to Miss Franny at the library
c. offering to sweep, dust, and take out the trash at the store
d. cleaning the pews at the church

Initials

3 What was the reason Otis offered Opal a job?

a. Opal convinced Otis she was smart.
b. The bird squawked, "*DOG!*"
c. Opal said she didn't need to be paid.
d. Her dad was a preacher.

Initials

4 What did Sweetie Pie do that made Opal feel less lonely?

a. asked her to go to the library with her
b. talked to her about the dog she was getting
c. invited Opal to her birthday party
d. said she didn't have a mom either

Initials

5 How did the Dewberry boys describe Gloria Dump?

a. a dog-eating witch
b. cranky old lady who loved children
c. sweet lady who shared peanut butter sandwiches
d. weird and mysterious grandmother

Initials

6 What conclusion can you make about how Opal feels about her last name, Buloni?

a. She thinks it is interesting and clever.
b. She dislikes it because other students called her "lunch meat."
c. She wishes she had her father's last name.
d. It's all she has from her mother.

Initials

7 What did Gloria rely on since she had poor eyesight?

a. a sight-seeing dog
b. strong prescription glasses
c. her heart
d. feeling with her fingers

Initials

8 What does the phrase "*green thumb*" mean?

a. thumb that has an infection
b. good gardener
c. painted thumb
d. having a thumb worth green polish

Initials

9 What kind of tree did Opal plant at Gloria's?

a. an ever-growing tree
b. ghost chaser tree
c. wait-and-see tree
d. worries-be-gone tree

Initials

Recall Questions
Because of Winn-Dixie • Chapters 11–16

Directions: Participate in Find Someone Who to answer the recall questions about *Because of Winn-Dixie*. Circle the correct answer provided by your partner and have your partner initial the answer.

1 What was Winn-Dixie's pathological fear?

a. spiders
b. thunderstorms
c. hairbrushes
d. baths

_____
Initials

2 What did Opal notice when she arrived for her first day at the job?

a. The shop was still locked and closed.
b. Gertrude, the owner, was visiting.
c. The red leather leash and collar were gone.
d. Otis was playing his guitar for the animals.

_____
Initials

3 Why did Otis feel sorry for the animals?

a. They were being sold to different families.
b. The mother animals had to say goodbye to their babies.
c. Otis knew what it was like to be locked up.
d. He loved the animals and didn't want them to go.

_____
Initials

4 How did Opal know Gloria Dump's house was Winn-Dixie's favorite place to visit?

a. He would start to lick his lips when they got closer.
b. He would break away from her bike and run.
c. He would start shaking with excitement.
d. He started to bark wildly.

_____
Initials

5 What advice did Gloria give Opal about how to deal with the Dewberry boys' bullying?

a. Opal should take a different route to her house.
b. She should ignore them and they would leave her alone.
c. She should try to be their friends.
d. She should tell Preacher.

_____
Initials

6 What was unique about Gloria's backyard tree?

a. It had twinkling lights strung all around it.
b. There were bottles hanging from the branches.
c. She had numerous bird feeders and birdhouses in the leaves.
d. Pictures of her favorite times were hung up.

_____
Initials

7 What did Miss Franny recommend Opal read to Gloria?

a. *Gone with the Wind*
b. *Great Expectations*
c. *The Scarlet Letter*
d. *Moby Dick*

_____
Initials

8 How old was Littmus when he enlisted in the war?

a. 18
b. 14
c. 16
d. 21

_____
Initials

9 What did Littmus find when he returned from the war?

a. His loving family waiting for him.
b. His town was destroyed from the war bombs.
c. His family had died and his house was burned down.
d. His family moved to be safer.

_____
Initials

Cooperative Learning & Literature
Kagan Publishing • (800) 933-2667 • www.KaganOnline.com

Recall Questions
Because of Winn-Dixie • Chapters 17–21

Directions: Participate in Find Someone Who to answer the recall questions about *Because of Winn-Dixie*. Circle the correct answer provided by your partner and have your partner initial the answer.

1 What was Littmus' plan to add something sweet to the world?

a. build a candy factory
b. sing soothing music
c. write a book about the positive part of wars
d. create a book of poetry

_____ Initials

2 What was special about the Littmus Lozenge?

a. It was created using only vegetables.
b. It made the eaters feel sad.
c. It brought joy to those who ate it.
d. It changes color as you eat it.

_____ Initials

3 What was Opal's reason for reading Gone with the Wind to Gloria?

a. She wanted Gloria to be her friend.
b. She wanted to teach Gloria about the wind.
c. She wanted to keep her ghosts away.
d. She didn't want her to be lonely.

_____ Initials

4 What was the cause of Amanda Wilkinson's sorrow?

a. She didn't have any friends.
b. Her parents are getting a divorce.
c. Her brother drowned the year before.
d. She lost her dog at the beginning of the summer.

_____ Initials

5 Why did Otis spend time in jail?

a. He stole his guitar from a music store.
b. He sang his songs on the street and refused to stop.
c. He didn't pay a ticket for street singing.
d. He hit a customer who refused to pay for his music.

_____ Initials

6 What promise did Opal make Gloria in order to have the party?

a. She would invite the Dewberry boys.
b. She would make egg salad sandwiches.
c. She would bring Winn-Dixie.
d. She would ask Otis to play his music.

_____ Initials

7 What theme did Sweetie Pie suggest for the party?

a. pink and yellow
b. friendship
c. dogs
d. music and pickles

_____ Initials

8 Why did Gloria want the party to be at night?

a. It would be cooler.
b. They would be able to see the lightening bugs.
c. The stars would be a nice decoration.
d. Everyone would be off work.

_____ Initials

9 What did Otis bring to the party?

a. pickles
b. CD of his music
c. his favorite dessert
d. egg salad sandwiches

_____ Initials

Recall Questions
Because of Winn-Dixie • Chapters 22–26

Directions: Participate in Find Someone Who to answer the recall questions about *Because of Winn-Dixie*. Circle the correct answer provided by your partner and have your partner initial the answer.

1 What happened after the rain started pouring down?

a. Everyone went home.
b. Winn-Dixie couldn't be found.
c. All the bottles fell off the tree.
d. The party continued in the rain.

Initials _____

2 What was the first item on Opal's list of things she knew about Winn-Dixie?

a. He loves peanut butter.
b. He sneezes when he smiles.
c. He has a pathological fear of thunderstorms.
d. He doesn't like to be left alone.

Initials _____

3 What was the most important thing that Opal's mother left behind?

a. Winn-Dixie
b. her Bible
c. her favorite jewelry
d. Opal

Initials _____

4 What was the first thing Opal noticed after returning to the party?

a. The rain had stopped.
b. Everyone was singing.
c. Only Gloria remained.
d. Winn-Dixie was sitting in Sweetie Pie's lap.

Initials _____

5 Where was Winn-Dixie while Opal was searching for him?

a. at their trailer
b. behind Opal's tree
c. under Gloria's bed
d. on the porch of the church

Initials _____

6 What gesture did Dunlap do that surprised Opal?

a. He kissed her on the cheek.
b. He hugged her to help her stay warm.
c. He offered his hand to help her up.
d. He shook her hand as a way to thank her for inviting him.

Initials _____

7 Why was Opal reluctant to sing?

a. She didn't know any songs.
b. She didn't think she had a good singing voice.
c. She enjoyed watching everyone else have a good time.
d. She didn't want to let go of Winn-Dixie.

Initials _____

8 What lesson can you learn after reading this book?

a. You need to take care of dogs with pathological fears or they will run away forever.
b. You can't hold onto something that wants to go, only love it while you have it.
c. You shouldn't care about people who have left you.

Initials _____

9 Why did the author most likely write this story?

a. to teach the reader how to take care of a dog afraid of storms
b. to persuade the reader to find more friends
c. to entertain the reader about a girl who makes unlikely friends

Initials _____

Cooperative Learning & Literature
Kagan Publishing • (800) 933-2667 • www.KaganOnline.com

Recall Questions
Because of Winn-Dixie • End-of-Book

Directions: Copy one set of cards for each team. Cut out each card along the dotted line. Give each team a set of cards to play Fan-N-Pick or Showdown.

---

① Because of Winn-Dixie

What did Gloria Dump have Opal do to see if she had a green thumb?

Fan-N-Pick/Showdown

---

② Because of Winn-Dixie

Where was Winn-Dixie found after he disappeared from the party?

Fan-N-Pick/Showdown

---

③ Because of Winn-Dixie

What was the first thing Winn-Dixie did when he went into the trailer to meet the Preacher?

Fan-N-Pick/Showdown

---

④ Because of Winn-Dixie

What was the tenth thing that the Preacher told Opal about her mother?

Fan-N-Pick/Showdown

---

⑤ Because of Winn-Dixie

What did Otis promise not to do once he was released from jail?

Fan-N-Pick/Showdown

---

⑥ Because of Winn-Dixie

What inspired Winn-Dixie's name?

Fan-N-Pick/Showdown

---

⑦ Because of Winn-Dixie

What was Winn-Dixie's pathological fear?

Fan-N-Pick/Showdown

---

⑧ Because of Winn-Dixie

What did Sweetie Pie Thomas do that made Opal feel less lonely in Naomi?

Fan-N-Pick/Showdown

Recall Questions
Because of Winn-Dixie • End-of-Book

Directions: Copy one set of cards for each team. Cut out each card along the dotted line. Give each team a set of cards to play Fan-N-Pick or Showdown.

---

⑨ Because of Winn-Dixie

What book did Opal check out from the library to read to Gloria?

Fan-N-Pick/Showdown

---

⑩ Because of Winn-Dixie

How did Miss Franny Block become librarian?

Fan-N-Pick/Showdown

---

⑪ Because of Winn-Dixie

Why did Amanda look "pinched-face"?

Fan-N-Pick/Showdown

---

⑫ Because of Winn-Dixie

What candy did Miss Franny's great-grandfather create?

Fan-N-Pick/Showdown

---

⑬ Because of Winn-Dixie

What was one thing Opal's mother did not do well?

Fan-N-Pick/Showdown

---

⑭ Because of Winn-Dixie

What did Winn-Dixie do when he smiled big?

Fan-N-Pick/Showdown

---

⑮ Because of Winn-Dixie

What did the Dewberry boys think of Gloria?

Fan-N-Pick/Showdown

---

⑯ Because of Winn-Dixie

What section of the grocery store was Winn-Dixie in when Opal found him?

Fan-N-Pick/Showdown

Cooperative Learning & Literature
Kagan Publishing • (800) 933-2667 • www.KaganOnline.com

Journal Writing
Because of Winn-Dixie • Beginning-of-Book

Directions: Think about the Journal Question, and then write your own response. When done, RoundRobin share your writing with your teammates. Use the space at the bottom to record ideas your teammates share.

Journal Question
Why is Opal lonely in Naomi? Make a connection to a time you felt alone below.

Journal Response: _____
_____
_____
_____
_____
_____
_____
_____
_____
_____
_____

Ideas Teammates Shared

Journal Writing
Because of Winn-Dixie • Middle-of-Book

Directions: Think about the Journal Question, and then write your own response. When done, RoundRobin share your writing with your teammates. Use the space at the bottom to record ideas your teammates share.

Journal Question
Gloria tells Opal that the Dewberry boys are mean to her because they want to be her friend. Why are some people mean to those they want to have as friends?

Journal Response: _____

_____

_____

_____

_____

_____

_____

_____

_____

_____

_____

Ideas Teammates Shared

Cooperative Learning & Literature
Kagan Publishing • (800) 933-2667 • www.KaganOnline.com

Journal Writing
Because of Winn-Dixie • End-of-Book

Directions: Think about the Journal Question, and then write your own response. When done, RoundRobin share your writing with your teammates. Use the space at the bottom to record ideas your teammates share.

Journal Question
How does Opal change from the beginning of the story to the end of the story? Explain.

Journal Response: _____

_____

_____

_____

_____

_____

_____

_____

_____

_____

_____

_____

Ideas Teammates Shared

Higher-Level Thinking Cards
Because of Winn-Dixie

Directions: Copy enough cards so that each student receives a Question Card. Have students stand up, pair up, and do Traveling Pair Share to respond to each other's questions. Students trade cards and find a new partner to share.

① Because of Winn-Dixie

Why does Opal feel lonely in Naomi? How does this change throughout the story?

Traveling Pair Share

② Because of Winn-Dixie

What characteristics best describe Opal? Explain.

Traveling Pair Share

③ Because of Winn-Dixie

How does Preacher's relationship with Opal change from the beginning to the end of the story?

Traveling Pair Share

④ Because of Winn-Dixie

Was it a good or bad decision for Opal to work at Gertrude's Pets? Explain.

Traveling Pair Share

⑤ Because of Winn-Dixie

What lesson does Opal learn in the story? Explain.

Traveling Pair Share

⑥ Because of Winn-Dixie

Explain why Opal calls Amanda "pinched-face." How does her opinion change after she learns about her brother?

Traveling Pair Share

⑦ Because of Winn-Dixie

How would the story be different if Winn-Dixie wasn't afraid of storms? Explain.

Traveling Pair Share

⑧ Because of Winn-Dixie

What does Gloria mean when she tells Opal, "*You can't hold on to things that want to go; you just have to love it while you have it?*"

Traveling Pair Share

Cooperative Learning & Literature
Kagan Publishing • (800) 933-2667 • www.KaganOnline.com

Higher-Level Thinking Cards
Because of Winn-Dixie

Directions: Copy enough cards so that each student receives a Question Card. Have students stand up, pair up, and do Traveling Pair Share to respond to each other's questions. Students trade cards and find a new partner to share.

⑨ Because of Winn-Dixie

If you were invited to Opal's party, what would you bring and why?

Traveling Pair Share

⑩ Because of Winn-Dixie

If you wanted to learn more about the Civil War, where would you look for information?

Traveling Pair Share

⑪ Because of Winn-Dixie

The Preacher told Opal that her mother left because she didn't like being a preacher's wife. Explain what he means.

Traveling Pair Share

⑫ Because of Winn-Dixie

What similarities can you find between yourself and Opal?

Traveling Pair Share

⑬ Because of Winn-Dixie

What predications can you make about the relationships after the party?

Traveling Pair Share

⑭ Because of Winn-Dixie

What is the significance of Opal bathing and grooming Winn-Dixie after adopting him?

Traveling Pair Share

⑮ Because of Winn-Dixie

How is the setting of the small town of Naomi important to the story? Explain.

Traveling Pair Share

⑯ Because of Winn-Dixie

On a scale of 1 to 10, how would you rate Opal's decision to throw a party for her new friends? Explain.

Traveling Pair Share

Higher-Level Thinking Cards
Because of Winn-Dixie

Directions: Copy enough cards so that each student receives a Question Card. Have students stand up, pair up, and do Traveling Pair Share to respond to each other's questions. Students trade cards and find a new partner to share.

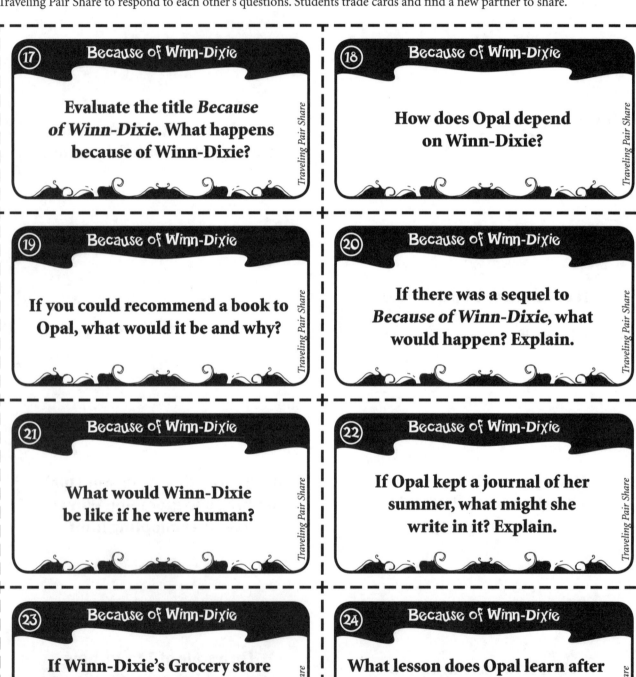

17 Because of Winn-Dixie

Evaluate the title *Because of Winn-Dixie*. What happens because of Winn-Dixie?

Traveling Pair Share

18 Because of Winn-Dixie

How does Opal depend on Winn-Dixie?

Traveling Pair Share

19 Because of Winn-Dixie

If you could recommend a book to Opal, what would it be and why?

Traveling Pair Share

20 Because of Winn-Dixie

If there was a sequel to *Because of Winn-Dixie*, what would happen? Explain.

Traveling Pair Share

21 Because of Winn-Dixie

What would Winn-Dixie be like if he were human?

Traveling Pair Share

22 Because of Winn-Dixie

If Opal kept a journal of her summer, what might she write in it? Explain.

Traveling Pair Share

23 Because of Winn-Dixie

If Winn-Dixie's Grocery store manager had caught Winn-Dixie, how might the story have changed?

Traveling Pair Share

24 Because of Winn-Dixie

What lesson does Opal learn after she invites so many different types of people to the party?

Traveling Pair Share

Cooperative Learning & Literature
Kagan Publishing • (800) 933-2667 • www.KaganOnline.com

The Boxcar Children

By Gertrude Chandler Warner

O rphans, Henry, Jessie, Violet, and Benny find themselves on the run from a grandfather whom they have never met before. Set in the 1940s, these four children find a home for themselves in an abandoned boxcar out in the woods. The boxcar provides the perfect shelter from animals at night and storms overhead. Jessie helps a dog with a thorn in his paw and the dog stays with them and protects them; they name him Watch. Henry, the oldest, finds work in town with the local doctor and earns money to purchase the necessities such as milk, bread, and cheese. The four children are unaware of the doctor's watchful eyes and of their grandfather's ad to find his missing grandchildren. Eventually, the doctor is able to reunite the children and grandfather and all of them discover how wonderful it is to have a family.

Reading Level
Lexile Level: 490L
Guided Reading Level: O
DRA Level: 34
Accelerated Reader: 3.2

The Boxcar Children

~ Cooperative Learning Activities ~

Recall Questions
The Boxcar Children • Chapters 1–2

❏ **RallyCoach Directions:** Take turns answering each question as your partner coaches. Explain your thinking to your coach.

❏ **Sage-N-Scribe Directions:** The Sage describes what he or she knows about the question so the Scribe can answer the question. The Sage and Scribe switch roles for each question.

Name _____

1. **When does this story take place?**
   a. the future
   b. the past
   c. the present

2. **Why did the baker not want to keep Benny and planned to send him to the children's home?**
   a. He was a little boy and too young.
   b. She already had enough children at home.
   c. She did not like Benny and he would be a lot of work.
   d. Benny already ate too much.

3. **What conclusion can you make about the reason the children walk during the night?**
   a. They can see better at night.
   b. It is too cold during the day.
   c. They do not want to be seen by others.
   d. Benny is afraid of the sunlight.

4. **What did the children eat for dinner after their night spent walking?**
   a. fresh eggs and fish
   b. a handful of nuts
   c. hay from the barn
   d. a piece of bread and water

5. **What did the children discover by the side of the road?**
   a. a lost horse
   b. a bag with towels and sheets
   c. a drinking fountain
   d. a pair of boots

Name _____

1. **Where did the children sleep the first night?**
   a. a haystack behind the farmer's market
   b. a bed of pine needles in a wagon
   c. a red bench at the bakery
   d. a bed at the children's home

2. **Why did the children not want to meet their grandfather?**
   a. The grandfather did not like their mother.
   b. The grandfather was sick.
   c. The grandfather did not like children.
   d. The grandfather lived too far away.

3. **What animal did Violet suggest Benny pretend to be so he would walk faster?**
   a. bear
   b. fish
   c. cheetah
   d. dog

4. **What caused the children to head towards Silver City rather than Greenfield?**
   a. The grandfather was in Greenfield.
   b. The baker was going to Greenfield.
   c. Violet did not want to walk that far.
   d. Jessie was afraid they would get lost.

5. **Why were the children not able to hear the thunder?**
   a. The thunder was far away.
   b. The sky was sunny and clear.
   c. They decided to walk the other way.
   d. They were fast asleep.

Recall Questions
The Boxcar Children • Chapters 3–4

❑ **RallyCoach Directions:** Take turns answering each question as your partner coaches. Explain your thinking to your coach.

❑ **Sage-N-Scribe Directions:** The Sage describes what he or she knows about the question so the Scribe can answer the question. The Sage and Scribe switch roles for each question.

Name _____

1. Where did the children find a new home in which to live?
a. an abandoned farm house
b. an old boxcar in the woods
c. a spot in a chicken nest
d. a tree house up in the forest

2. Who decided the boxcar needed to look more like a home?
a. Violet
b. Jessie
c. Benny
d. Henry

3. Where did the children wash up before dinner?
a. the bathroom sink
b. at a gas station down the road
c. a well in the woods
d. a brook near the boxcar

4. What was the cause of the noise heard in the woods?
a. a dog walking with a sore paw
b. Henry leaving to get milk
c. a stranger nearby
d. Benny throwing rocks away

5. What conclusion can you make about the new pet?
a. Henry will be upset because he does not like dogs.
b. The dog is very gentle and kind.
c. The dog will bite one of the children.
d. The dog likes to play in water.

Name _____

1. What did the children use as stairs to get into their new home?
a. a turned over wagon
b. a large, moss-covered stone
c. a tree stump
d. a pile of dry needles

2. Why did Benny not want to stay in their new home?
a. He thought they would be easy to find.
b. He did not like being alone in the dark.
c. He was afraid the engine would come back.
d. He missed their grandfather.

3. What did Jessie see in the woods that would be good to eat?
a. wild mushrooms
b. blueberries
c. fresh fish
d. wild strawberries

4. Who helped remove the thorn from the dog's paw?
a. Benny
b. Jessie
c. Violet
d. Henry

5. Which of the following is NOT something Henry bought while in town?
a. a tin cup
b. four bottles of milk
c. brown bread
d. fine yellow cheese

Cooperative Learning & Literature
Kagan Publishing • (800) 933-2667 • www.KaganOnline.com

Recall Questions
The Boxcar Children • Chapters 5–6

❏ **RallyCoach Directions:** Take turns answering each question as your partner coaches. Explain your thinking to your coach.

❏ **Sage-N-Scribe Directions:** The Sage describes what he or she knows about the question so the Scribe can answer the question. The Sage and Scribe switch roles for each question.

Name _____

1. What did Jessie use as a refrigerator to keep the milk cool?
a. a dark hole in the cave
b. a spot behind a small waterfall
c. an ice chest in the boxcar
d. behind a stack of rocks in the shade

2. What special treasure did Benny find for himself?
a. a rusty wagon
b. a worn out teddy bear
c. a small bowl and matching plate
d. a cracked pink cup

3. What did Henry bring for Watch after working for the doctors?
a. dog treats
b. a bone
c. a new toy
d. a collar and leash

4. What did the cook give Henry before leaving the doctor's house?
a. milk and bread
b. bacon and eggs
c. bag of cookies
d. spices

5. What caused Watch to growl during the night?
a. A deer was drinking from the brook.
b. Benny was lost in the woods.
c. A rabbit was eating the vegetables.
d. He heard a stick crack in the woods.

Name _____

1. Where did the children find tin cups, wheels, and a pitcher?
a. the general store
b. a neighbor's house
c. a dump
d. in a cabinet in the boxcar

2. How did Jessie make sure the new dishes were clean enough to use to eat?
a. She cleaned them with soap.
b. She scrubbed them with sand.
c. She placed them into the fire.
d. She rinsed them with boiling water.

3. What work did Henry find in town?
a. mowing a lawn
b. milking the cows
c. washing laundry
d. stocking shelves

4. What special treat did Henry bring back for Jessie?
a. a new skirt
b. yellow sweet butter
c. a pitcher of tea
d. a bar of soap

5. What conclusion can you make about the reason Watch laid down and went to sleep?
a. Jessie scratched his ears.
b. Watch was no longer worried.
c. Henry returned to the boxcar.
d. Watch was very tired.

Recall Questions
The Boxcar Children • Chapters 7–8

❏ **RallyCoach Directions:** Take turns answering each question as your partner coaches. Explain your thinking to your coach.

❏ **Sage-N-Scribe Directions:** The Sage describes what he or she knows about the question so the Scribe can answer the question. The Sage and Scribe switch roles for each question.

Name _____

1. **What job did Mrs. Moore give Henry?**
a. washing the pots and pans
b. thinning out the vegetable garden
c. planting flowers
d. moving boxes out of the house

2. **What did Benny build with stones?**
a. a small house
b. a fireplace
c. a table
d. steps to the boxcar

3. **What did Henry collect in his pockets?**
a. extra hammers
b. seeds for a garden
c. pieces of leftover food
d. bent nails

4. **What did Jessie do while the others worked?**
a. fixed the cracked kettle
b. swept out the boxcar
c. washed the stockings
d. built a fire

5. **What did the children find in the woods that they ate for supper?**
a. wild mushrooms
b. hen eggs
c. ripe tomatoes
d. juicy, red apples

Name _____

1. **What conclusion can you make about why Mrs. Moore was looking out the window?**
a. She did not like Henry.
b. She was afraid of Henry.
c. She did not trust Henry.
d. She was curious about Henry.

2. **Why was cleaning the garage fun for Henry?**
a. He likes to look at different tools.
b. He likes to build furniture.
c. He likes to get things in order.
d. He likes to help others.

3. **What did the children build on Sunday?**
a. a cooking area
b. a swimming pool
c. a laundry area
d. a set of stairs

4. **Why did the stew taste even better the second night?**
a. Jessie added more salt.
b. Henry made fresh bread.
c. Benny said a special prayer.
d. The children had worked really hard.

5. **What did Jessie use to make supper?**
a. a black kettle
b. new pots and pans
c. a stove in the boxcar
d. warm water and luck

Cooperative Learning & Literature
Kagan Publishing • (800) 933-2667 • www.KaganOnline.com

Recall Questions
The Boxcar Children • Chapters 9–10

❏ **RallyCoach Directions:** Take turns answering each question as your partner coaches. Explain your thinking to your coach.

❏ **Sage-N-Scribe Directions:** The Sage describes what he or she knows about the question so the Scribe can answer the question. The Sage and Scribe switch roles for each question.

Name _____

1. What did the children worry about while going to the cherry orchard?
a. losing Benny
b. Grandfather seeing them
c. Dr. Moore finding out where they lived
d. Violet getting tired

2. What was Dr. Moore's reason for giving Henry four dollars?
a. Henry will work four more days.
b. Benny wanted to take home some cherries.
c. Violet needed a new pair of shoes.
d. The children were so happy while working.

3. What special event does J. H. Alden give each year?
a. Field Day
b. Pie Eating Contest
c. Horse Races
d. Barn Dance

4. Why did Henry not give his whole name after he won the race?
a. He knew he would not keep the money.
b. He did not want anyone to know his last name.
c. He did not like his last name.
d. He would be arrested for cheating.

5. Why did Benny decide he would learn to read?
a. He liked to read books.
b. He wanted to work like Henry.
c. He would not let Watch be a better reader.
d. He did not want to be forced to go to school.

Name _____

1. What was Benny's job at the orchard?
a. helping Mrs. Moore with the ladder
b. carrying water for Jessie and Violet
c. watching for trees with lots of cherries
d. carrying and filling little baskets

2. Where did Dr. Moore read about four lost children?
a. a poster
b. a letter at the post office
c. a newspaper
d. the side of the mill

3. What conclusion can you make about the reason Dr. Moore sent Henry to the race?
a. Henry could earn extra money for Dr. Moore.
b. Henry needed to learn to work harder.
c. Henry's grandfather gave out the prize money.
d. Henry had already finished the garage.

4. What did Henry do with his prize money?
a. gave it to the doctor for the vegetables
b. bought a new pillow for Benny
c. gave it to Jessie
d. bought new stockings for everyone

5. How did Jessie cook the potatoes?
a. using a fire under the hot stones
b. in boiling water
c. in the warm, hot sun
d. in a pan over the fire

Recall Questions
The Boxcar Children • Chapters 11–13

❏ **RallyCoach Directions:** Take turns answering each question as your partner coaches. Explain your thinking to your coach.

❏ **Sage-N-Scribe Directions:** The Sage describes what he or she knows about the question so the Scribe can answer the question. The Sage and Scribe switch roles for each question.

Name _____

1. **What did the girls make for Benny?**
   a. a marble game
   b. a bear out of stockings
   c. a fluffy pillow
   d. a desk and chair

2. **Why did Jessie think Violet was sick?**
   a. Violet would not eat.
   b. Violet had slept all day.
   c. Violet could not stop crying.
   d. Violet did not want to work.

3. **What conclusion can you make about the reason Dr. Moore stayed up with Violet all night?**
   a. Violet was very sick.
   b. Dr. Moore thought she would run away.
   c. Violet could not go to sleep.
   d. Henry was worried Dr. Moore would leave.

4. **Why was Benny unable to run the train all day?**
   a. The train did not have enough tracks.
   b. Mr. Alden would be gone during the day.
   c. Benny would have to go to school.
   d. The train did not belong to Mr. Alden.

5. **What solution did Henry suggest for keeping Watch?**
   a. Henry would wash him every day.
   b. Violet would offer to babysit the neighbor.
   c. Benny would walk Watch after school.
   d. Ask the lady if she would be willing to take another dog.

Name _____

1. **What did Benny do while cutting Watch's hair?**
   a. cut a J on one side
   b. sang him a song
   c. collected the loose hair
   d. told him about his parents

2. **Why were the children uneasy about taking Violet to the hospital?**
   a. They did not have enough money.
   b. They would have to tell them their names.
   c. Their grandfather worked as a doctor.
   d. Henry did not know where to find a hospital.

3. **Why did Dr. Moore know about the children's boxcar?**
   a. Henry told Dr. Moore about his home.
   b. Dr. Moore followed Henry home one night.
   c. The boxcar belonged to Dr. Moore's mom.
   d. Mr. Alden used the boxcar for camping.

4. **Where did Watch sleep after moving into Mr. Alden's house?**
   a. in a special dog house in the back yard
   b. on the floor next to Jessie's bed
   c. in his own special room
   d. with Henry in the basement

5. **What caused the children to laugh while at the dinner table?**
   a. Benny told Mr. Alden about the boxcar.
   b. Watch was being waited on by a maid.
   c. Violet spilled her milk.
   d. Mr. Alden announced they would move to the boxcar!

Cooperative Learning & Literature
Kagan Publishing • (800) 933-2667 • www.KaganOnline.com

Journal Writing
The Boxcar Children • Chapter 1

Directions: Think about the Journal Question, and then write your own response. When done, RoundRobin share your writing with your teammates. Use the space at the bottom to record ideas your teammates share.

Journal Question
Do you think it was a good decision for Henry, Jessie, Violet, and Benny to be on their own with no adults? Explain your thinking.

Journal Response: _____

_____
_____
_____
_____
_____
_____
_____
_____
_____
_____

Ideas Teammates Shared

Journal Writing
The Boxcar Children • Chapter 3

Directions: Think about the Journal Question, and then write your own response. When done, RoundRobin share your writing with your teammates. Use the space at the bottom to record ideas your teammates share.

Journal Question
How does finding the boxcar affect Henry, Jessie, Violet, and Benny?

Journal Response: _____

_____

_____

_____

_____

_____

_____

_____

_____

_____

_____

_____

Ideas Teammates Shared

Cooperative Learning & Literature
Kagan Publishing • (800) 933-2667 • www.KaganOnline.com

Journal Writing
The Boxcar Children • Chapter 5

Directions: Think about the Journal Question, and then write your own response. When done, RoundRobin share your writing with your teammates. Use the space at the bottom to record ideas your teammates share.

Journal Question
Do you think it is a good decision for the children to use
the items they find from the dump? Explain your thinking.

Journal Response: _____

_____

_____

_____

_____

_____

_____

_____

_____

_____

_____

_____

_____

Ideas Teammates Shared

Journal Writing
The Boxcar Children • Chapter 6

Directions: Think about the Journal Question, and then write your own response. When done, RoundRobin share your writing with your teammates. Use the space at the bottom to record ideas your teammates share.

Journal Question
How does Watch help protect the children? Why is this important?

Journal Response: _____

_____

_____

_____

_____

_____

_____

_____

_____

_____

_____

_____

Ideas Teammates Shared

Cooperative Learning & Literature
Kagan Publishing • (800) 933-2667 • www.KaganOnline.com

Journal Writing
The Boxcar Children • Chapter 7

Directions: Think about the Journal Question, and then write your own response. When done, RoundRobin share your writing with your teammates. Use the space at the bottom to record ideas your teammates share.

Journal Question
Benny cares a lot about his new cart and Henry cares a lot about his hammer.
Why are these simple items important?

Journal Response: _____

_____

_____

_____

_____

_____

_____

_____

_____

_____

_____

Ideas Teammates Shared

Journal Writing
The Boxcar Children • Chapter 9

Directions: Think about the Journal Question, and then write your own response. When done, RoundRobin share your writing with your teammates. Use the space at the bottom to record ideas your teammates share.

Journal Question
Do you think it was a good decision for Dr. Moore not to
tell Mr. Alden about his grandchildren?

Journal Response: _____

_____

_____

_____

_____

_____

_____

_____

_____

_____

_____

_____

Ideas Teammates Shared

Cooperative Learning & Literature
Kagan Publishing • (800) 933-2667 • www.KaganOnline.com

Journal Writing
The Boxcar Children • Chapter 11

Directions: Think about the Journal Question, and then write your own response. When done, RoundRobin share your writing with your teammates. Use the space at the bottom to record ideas your teammates share.

Journal Question
How has Dr. Moore helped the children survive alone in the boxcar? Explain your thinking.

Journal Response: _____

_____

_____

_____

_____

_____

_____

_____

_____

_____

_____

_____

Ideas Teammates Shared

Journal Writing
The Boxcar Children • Chapter 13

Directions: Think about the Journal Question, and then write your own response. When done, RoundRobin share your writing with your teammates. Use the space at the bottom to record ideas your teammates share.

Journal Question
What do you think will happen now that the children are living with
Mr. Alden and have their boxcar in their own backyard?

Journal Response: _____

_____

_____

_____

_____

_____

_____

_____

_____

_____

_____

Ideas Teammates Shared

Cooperative Learning & Literature
Kagan Publishing • (800) 933-2667 • www.KaganOnline.com

Journal Writing
The Boxcar Children • End-of-Book

Directions: Think about the Journal Question, and then write your own response. When done, RoundRobin share your writing with your teammates. Use the space at the bottom to record ideas your teammates share.

Journal Question
Imagine you are Mr. Alden and were looking for your grandchildren. What could you have done to locate Henry, Jessie, Violet, and Benny? Describe your plan of action.

Journal Response: _____

_____

_____

_____

_____

_____

_____

_____

_____

_____

_____

_____

Ideas Teammates Shared

Higher-Level Thinking Cards
The Boxcar Children

Directions: Copy enough cards so that each student receives a Question Card. Have students stand up, pair up, and do Traveling Pair Share to respond to each other's questions. Students trade cards and find a new partner to share.

① The Boxcar Children

Why are the children so afraid of their grandfather? How would the story be different if the grandfather found them sooner?

Traveling Pair Share

② The Boxcar Children

Why is it important for Jessie and Violet to make the boxcar feel like home?

Traveling Pair Share

③ The Boxcar Children

Does this story take place in the past, present, or future? What clues in the story help you determine the setting?

Traveling Pair Share

④ The Boxcar Children

What character traits describe Benny, Violet, Jessie, and Henry? Explain.

Traveling Pair Share

⑤ The Boxcar Children

Do you think the children would be able to survive for a long time in the boxcar? Explain and justify your answer.

Traveling Pair Share

⑥ The Boxcar Children

How are the four children in this story different from you? Explain.

Traveling Pair Share

⑦ The Boxcar Children

Why do you think Dr. Moore did not tell the children he knew they were living in boxcar?

Traveling Pair Share

⑧ The Boxcar Children

How might the children's lives change now that they are living with Mr. Alden?

Traveling Pair Share

Cooperative Learning & Literature
Kagan Publishing • (800) 933-2667 • www.KaganOnline.com

Higher-Level Thinking Cards
The Boxcar Children

Directions: Copy enough cards so that each student receives a Question Card. Have students stand up, pair up, and do Traveling Pair Share to respond to each other's questions. Students trade cards and find a new partner to share.

⑨ The Boxcar Children

How does Dr. Moore help the children survive?

Traveling Pair Share

⑩ The Boxcar Children

What would you enjoy most about living in a boxcar?

Traveling Pair Share

⑪ The Boxcar Children

Which child are you the most like? Different?

Traveling Pair Share

⑫ The Boxcar Children

Which child had the most responsibility? Justify your answer using details.

Traveling Pair Share

⑬ The Boxcar Children

What questions would you like to ask the author Gertrude Chandler Warner?

Traveling Pair Share

⑭ The Boxcar Children

If you had to choose between living in a boxcar or finding your grandfather, what would you choose and why?

Traveling Pair Share

⑮ The Boxcar Children

What was the most important thing to the children? Justify your answer.

Traveling Pair Share

⑯ The Boxcar Children

If you could go into the story, what would be one item you would give to Henry, Violet, Jessie, and Benny? Explain your thinking.

Traveling Pair Share

Higher-Level Thinking Cards
The Boxcar Children

Directions: Copy enough cards so that each student receives a Question Card. Have students stand up, pair up, and do Traveling Pair Share to respond to each other's questions. Students trade cards and find a new partner to share.

---

17 — The Boxcar Children

How would the story have been different if Watch didn't find the children?

Traveling Pair Share

---

18 — The Boxcar Children

Did the baker's wife have a good reason to want to send Benny to the children's home? Why or why not?

Traveling Pair Share

---

19 — The Boxcar Children

What impact did Dr. Moore and Mrs. Moore have on the lives of the four children?

Traveling Pair Share

---

20 — The Boxcar Children

What could the children have done rather than run away from their grandfather?

Traveling Pair Share

---

21 — The Boxcar Children

How do the children change from the beginning of the story to the end of the story?

Traveling Pair Share

---

22 — The Boxcar Children

What might have happened if Henry did not go and get Dr. Moore to help Violet?

Traveling Pair Share

---

23 — The Boxcar Children

How would the story have been different if Henry would not have been the leader of the children? Explain.

Traveling Pair Share

---

24 — The Boxcar Children

Why do you think Watch ran away from the wealthy lady?

Traveling Pair Share

Cooperative Learning & Literature
Kagan Publishing • (800) 933-2667 • www.KaganOnline.com

Frindle

By Andrew Clements

What is a frindle? In short, it is a word invented by fifth grader Nick Allen as a way to seek revenge against his dictionary-loving language arts teacher. But Nick doesn't realize the battle a frindle will have on the school, nor the impact of the frindle on his future. What starts out as an experiment with a few friends, turns out to be worldwide recognition that is out of Nick's control.

Reading Level
Lexile Level: 830
Guided Reading Level: R
DRA Level: 40
Accelerated Reader: 5.4

Frindle

～ Cooperative Learning Activities ～

Cooperative Learning & Literature
Kagan Publishing • (800) 933-2667 • www.KaganOnline.com

Recall Questions
Frindle • Chapters 1–4

❏ **RallyCoach Directions:** Take turns answering each question as your partner coaches. Explain your thinking to your coach.

❏ **Sage-N-Scribe Directions:** The Sage describes what he or she knows about the question so the Scribe can answer the question. The Sage and Scribe switch roles for each question.

Name _____

1. What did Nick do when he was in 3rd grade?
a. replace all the classroom's dictionaries with *The World's Biggest Pranks*
b. paint the teacher's chair purple
c. turned his classroom into a tropical island
d. won the school spelling bee

2. What did Mrs. Granger teach?
a. language arts
b. social studies
c. science
d. math

3. According to the story, what do all language arts teachers love to make their students do?
a. read boring books
b. practice handwriting
c. write long reports
d. use the dictionary

4. What word best describes Mrs. Granger?
a. loving
b. understanding
c. strict
d. heartless

5. What was Nick's family rule at home?
a. homework first
b. chores then homework
c. no TV during the school week
d. homework is to be done right after dinner

Name _____

1. What caused giggling during silent reading time in Mrs. Avery's class?
a. The whoopee cushion on Mrs. Avery's chair was funny.
b. Janet kept sneezing.
c. Thomas fell back in his chair.
d. Nick was screeching the word, *"peep."*

2. What special talent did the 5th graders think Mrs. Granger possessed?
a. eyes in the back of her head
b. x-ray vision
c. eyes that made students do as she asked
d. torturing students with homework

3. What was Mrs. Allen's reaction to the letter she received from Mrs. Granger?
a. pleased to have a teacher take her work seriously
b. annoyed at having to buy a dictionary
c. worried about future letters she would receive
d. happy to know her child would be working hard

4. How did Mrs. Granger respond to Nick's teacher-stopper question?
a. ignored it
b. answered it in one short sentence
c. assigned Nick a report
d. read a book about the subject

5. Where did Nick look for information to complete his assignment?
a. Internet
b. book about the origin of words
c. encyclopedia sets
d. asked his brother

Recall Questions
Frindle • Chapters 5–8

❏ **RallyCoach Directions:** Take turns answering each question as your partner coaches. Explain your thinking to your coach.

❏ **Sage-N-Scribe Directions:** The Sage describes what he or she knows about the question so the Scribe can answer the question. The Sage and Scribe switch roles for each question.

Name _____

1. What was Nick's main goal while giving his oral report?
  a. to bore the class
  b. impress his teacher
  c. waste as much time as possible
  d. teach the class how interesting words can be

2. What did gwagala mean to Nick's family when he was younger?
  a. Nick wanted to listen to his music.
  b. Nick wanted his favorite toy, a giraffe.
  c. Nick wanted to eat watermelon.
  d. Nick needed his diaper changed.

3. What was the first step of Nick's plan?
  a. ask for frindles at the Penny Pantry
  b. send classmates to the teacher asking for frindles
  c. compose an email using frindles
  d. wear a shirt that says, "I have my frindle, do you?"

4. What conclusion can you make about the way Mrs. Granger feels about the word frindle?
  a. thought it very clever for Nick to invent a word
  b. annoyed about the inappropriate use of a word
  c. disappointed in students who used the disgusting word
  d. impressed it caught on so quickly

5. What was the purpose of Nick writing his name and date on the back of the envelope?
  a. to identify who the letter was addressed to
  b. to prove when the letter was written and then never opened
  c. to show Mrs. Granger he could write in cursive
  d. to persuade others to read the letter

Name _____

1. What did Mrs. Granger do following Nick's report?
  a. treated him like a teacher's pet
  b. ignored him
  c. sent him to principal's office for acting out in class
  d. asked him to add more detail to his report

2. What is a frindle?
  a. an electronic device used to read books
  b. a word Nick made up to mean pen
  c. a friend that will do anything for you
  d. a fake fire starter

3. What was Mrs. Granger's reaction to Nick and John's disruption in class?
  a. assigned both boys detention
  b. asked Nick to stay after class
  c. forbid Nick and John from throwing pens
  d. told students they could only write with pencils

4. What genre is the story *Frindle*?
  a. nonfiction
  b. tall tail
  c. biography
  d. realistic fiction

5. What was the effect of Mrs. Granger keeping so many students after school?
  a. The superintendent fired Mrs. Granger.
  b. Mrs. Granger was suspended for 2 weeks.
  c. The principal went to talk with Mr. and Mrs. Allen.
  d. Nick was not allowed to go to school for 3 weeks.

Cooperative Learning & Literature
Kagan Publishing • (800) 933-2667 • www.KaganOnline.com

Recall Questions
Frindle • Chapters 9–11

❏ **RallyCoach Directions:** Take turns answering each question as your partner coaches. Explain your thinking to your coach.

❏ **Sage-N-Scribe Directions:** The Sage describes what he or she knows about the question so the Scribe can answer the question. The Sage and Scribe switch roles for each question.

Name _____

1. Who visited Mr. and Mrs. Allen at their home regarding what was happening at school?
a. Mrs. Granger
b. Nick
c. Mrs. Chatham
d. Bud Lawrence

2. What was Mrs. Allen's reaction during the visit?
a. Nick was trying to be funny.
b. The situation is serious and they would have a long talk with Nick that night.
c. The school was picking on their son.
d. It is an overreaction to an experiment with language.

3. Who is Judy Morgan?
a. the reporter for CNN news
b. a writer for *The Westfield Gazette*
c. the superintendent of Lincoln Elementary
d. a parent of one of the students assigned detention

4. How does the article describe what is happening at Lincoln Elementary?
a. a case of disrespect
b. an example of how education is failing
c. war of the words
d. the reason students love school

Name _____

1. According to the school principal, what is the real problem at school?
a. the lack of respect for authority
b. use of words that mean nonsense
c. Students not completing their assignments correctly
d. Mrs. Granger and Nick not getting along

2. What was Nick's argument in using the word frindle?
a. He was only trying to prove a point.
b. The word ain't is found in the dictionary.
c. It was an experiment to see if the word would be popular.
d. He wanted to teach Mrs. Granger a lesson.

3. Why would Mrs. Chatham not be able to prevent Judy Morgan from speaking to Mrs. Granger?
a. Judy is a former student.
b. America is a free country with a free press.
c. Judy is a concerned parent with rights.
d. The superintendent is able to speak with teachers.

4. What question did Nick's mother, the school superintendent, and Mrs. Chatham ask following the publication of the article?
a. "*What is going to happen next?*"
b. "*Did you really say all of these things?*"
c. "*How could you talk about it?*"
d. "*What is the meaning of this?*"

Recall Questions
Frindle • Chapters 12–13

❏ **RallyCoach Directions:** Take turns answering each question as your partner coaches. Explain your thinking to your coach.

❏ **Sage-N-Scribe Directions:** The Sage describes what he or she knows about the question so the Scribe can answer the question. The Sage and Scribe switch roles for each question.

Name _____

1. How did Nick change after the article was written?
- **a.** He became more popular at school.
- **b.** He was shy and awkward.
- **c.** He was known for his jokes and being smart.
- **d.** He became very quiet but kept inventing new words.

2. What did Nick's mom mean when she told him to mind his "Ps and Qs" during the interview?
- **a.** to watch what he said so he didn't offend anyone
- **b.** to not use any words that started with Ps and Qs
- **c.** to pause before answering any questions
- **d.** to be sure to say please and thank you

3. What was Nick's reason for making up the word frindle?
- **a.** He wanted to get revenge against Mrs. Granger for making him write a report on the first day.
- **b.** He wanted to prove he could invent a new word and win a bet with his friend, John.
- **c.** All words in the dictionary were made by people, so Nick wanted to see if it were true, and fun to do.

4. What was Bud's reason for giving Nick's dad a check?
- **a.** Bud wanted to pay Nick for agreeing to be interviewed.
- **b.** Bud owed Nick the money from the first 3 weeks' profit.
- **c.** It was a down payment for Nick to stop using the word.
- **d.** It was the first paycheck for writing a book with Bud.

Name _____

1. How did Nick's parents feel about the news article?
- **a.** pleased that Nick invented a brand-new word
- **b.** annoyed that the article made their son sad
- **c.** upset that it made the town hate Nick
- **d.** happy that they were mentioned as his parents

2. How are the words quiz and frindle alike?
- **a.** Both words were made by students.
- **b.** Both are words that mean something to write with.
- **c.** Both words were invented for no particular reason.
- **d.** Both words were created by a teacher.

3. What deal did Bud Lawrence want to make with Nick's father?
- **a.** Bud wanted to use the word frindle to sell and would give Nick 30 percent of profits.
- **b.** Nick would stop using the word frindle in the future.
- **c.** Nick could earn money by writing a book with him.
- **d.** Bud wanted to interview Nick and his family.

4. What was Bud Lawrence's cause of happiness?
- **a.** The book was on the New York Time's best seller list.
- **b.** All the merchandise with frindle was selling quickly.
- **c.** Bud's interview with Nick was making national headlines.
- **d.** The word frindle was no longer popular.

Cooperative Learning & Literature
Kagan Publishing • (800) 933-2667 • www.KaganOnline.com

Recall Questions
Frindle • Chapters 14–15

❏ **RallyCoach Directions:** Take turns answering each question as your partner coaches. Explain your thinking to your coach.

❏ **Sage-N-Scribe Directions:** The Sage describes what he or she knows about the question so the Scribe can answer the question. The Sage and Scribe switch roles for each question.

Name _____

1. What conclusion can you make about Mrs. Granger's feelings toward Nick during their meeting on the last day of school?
 a. She despised his actions during the school year.
 b. She enjoyed having him as a student and expects great things from him in the future.
 c. She would be happy for him to go to 6th grade.
 d. She would never have a student as great as Nick.

2. What was special about the dictionary Mrs. Granger gave to Nick?
 a. It was hers when she was a student.
 b. It was the dictionary Nick used while in her class.
 c. It contained the word frindle.
 d. Mrs. Granger wrote Nick a note on the front cover.

3. What was the true reason Mrs. Granger fought against the use of the word frindle?
 a. She had actually helped the word become popular.
 b. She wanted to be sure her name was remembered when the story was retold later.
 c. She didn't want a student to be smarter.
 d. She knew it would never work.

4. What did Nick send Mrs. Granger for Christmas?
 a. a special red frindle with her name in gold writing
 b. a gold fountain pen with an inscription from Nick
 c. a check with half of his profits from frindle
 d. a signed copy of a dictionary with the word frindle

Name _____

1. What happened when Nick turned 21 years old?
 a. Nick's father delivered Nick a check for all the money frindle earned.
 b. Mrs. Granger visited Nick bringing him a dictionary.
 c. Nick received an award for inventing frindle.
 d. The frindle trust fund from frindle was legally Nicks.

2. What did Nick learn after reading Mrs. Granger's letter she wrote years ago?
 a. She was secretly hoping frindle would fail.
 b. She thought Nick was the best student she ever had in class.
 c. Nick reminded her of her son who died when he as young.
 d. She was purposely the villain for Nick's story.

3. What conclusion can you make about who set up The Lorelei Granger Students' Fund?
 a. It was Mrs. Chatham because she felt sorry for Mrs. Granger.
 b. It was Nick because he wanted a way to thank her.
 c. It was Judy Morgan as a way to apologize for her article.
 d. Mrs. Granger's former students wanted to show their appreciation.

4. How many years had Mrs. Granger taught school?
 a. 25 years
 b. 45 years
 c. 35 years
 d. 40 years

Recall Questions
Frindle • End-of-Book

Directions: Participate in Find Someone Who to answer the recall questions about *Frindle*. Write the answer in the space provided. Have your partner initial the answer.

1 Who was Mrs. Granger?

_____
_____
_____
_____
Initials

2 What did Mrs. Granger tell all parents their 5th graders would need?

_____
_____
_____
_____
Initials

3 Why were students kept after school and made to write 100 sentences?

_____
_____
_____
_____
Initials

4 What did the 5th grade class do during their group picture?

_____
_____
_____
_____
Initials

5 What did Nick learn after reading Mrs. Granger's letter?

_____
_____
_____
_____
Initials

6 What did Mrs. Granger do after Nick tried a teacher-stopper, or time-waster, question during his first language arts class?

_____
_____
_____
Initials

7 What did Bud Lawrence want to do with the word frindle?

_____
_____
_____
_____
Initials

8 Who was Judy Morgan?

_____
_____
_____
_____
Initials

9 What did Nick send Mrs. Granger for Christmas once he was in college?

_____
_____
_____
_____
Initials

10 What did Nick do during silent reading that he learned from "the Great Blackbird Discovery"?

_____
_____
_____
_____
Initials

11 What does the word frindle mean?

_____
_____
_____
_____
Initials

12 What was special about the dictionary Mrs. Granger sent to Nick when he was in college?

_____
_____
_____
_____
Initials

Cooperative Learning & Literature
Kagan Publishing • (800) 933-2667 • www.KaganOnline.com

Journal Writing
Frindle • Beginning-of-Book

Directions: Think about the Journal Question, and then write your own response. When done, RoundRobin share your writing with your teammates. Use the space at the bottom to record ideas your teammates share.

Journal Question
What qualities make a great teacher? What qualities make a bad teacher?
Explain and describe these qualities.

Journal Response: _____

_____

_____

_____

_____

_____

_____

_____

_____

_____

_____

_____

Ideas Teammates Shared

Journal Writing
Frindle • Middle-of-Book

Directions: Think about the Journal Question, and then write your own response. When done, RoundRobin share your writing with your teammates. Use the space at the bottom to record ideas your teammates share.

Journal Question
Think of an object at home or school. If you could invent a new name for it, what would it be? Why did you choose that name? Explain.

Journal Response: _____

_____

_____

_____

_____

_____

_____

_____

_____

_____

_____

_____

_____

Ideas Teammates Shared

Cooperative Learning & Literature
Kagan Publishing • (800) 933-2667 • www.KaganOnline.com

Journal Writing
Frindle • Middle-of-Book

Directions: Think about the Journal Question, and then write your own response. When done, RoundRobin share your writing with your teammates. Use the space at the bottom to record ideas your teammates share.

Journal Question
Why does Nick tell his father, "*It's a real word now. It used to be just mine, but not anymore.*"? Could Nick stop people from using the word? Why or why not? Explain.

Journal Response: _____

_____

_____

_____

_____

_____

_____

_____

_____

_____

_____

Ideas Teammates Shared

Journal Writing
Frindle • Middle-of-Book

Directions: Think about the Journal Question, and then write your own response. When done, RoundRobin share your writing with your teammates. Use the space at the bottom to record ideas your teammates share.

Journal Question
If Mrs. Granger had accepted the new word instead of fighting against it, how might the story be different? Explain.

Journal Response: _____

_____

_____

_____

_____

_____

_____

_____

_____

_____

_____

_____

Ideas Teammates Shared

Cooperative Learning & Literature
Kagan Publishing • (800) 933-2667 • www.KaganOnline.com

Journal Writing
Frindle • End-of-Book

Directions: Think about the Journal Question, and then write your own response. When done, RoundRobin share your writing with your teammates. Use the space at the bottom to record ideas your teammates share.

Journal Question
What did Nick learn about his experience with the invention of frindle that could help him as an adult?

Journal Response: _____

_____

_____

_____

_____

_____

_____

_____

_____

_____

_____

_____

Ideas Teammates Shared

Higher-Level Thinking Cards
Frindle

Directions: Copy enough cards so that each student receives a Question Card. Have students stand up, pair up, and do Traveling Pair Share to respond to each other's questions. Students trade cards and find a new partner to share.

① Frindle
Think about other words that did not exist 5 years ago. Share them with me.

② Frindle
How would the story be different if Mrs. Granger accepted the use of the word frindle?

③ Frindle
If you wanted to find out more about a word, where would you look? Explain.

④ Frindle
What are some words or phrases that you use with your friends? Would these words be found in a dictionary?

⑤ Frindle
If you were asked to interview Mrs. Granger or Nick about what happened 10 years ago during the "war of words," what questions would you ask? Explain.

⑥ Frindle
How does Nick change from the beginning of his 5th grade year to the end? Describe the changes.

⑦ Frindle
Do you agree or disagree with Mrs. Granger's decision to punish students for using the word frindle?

⑧ Frindle
What impact does Bud Lawrence have on Nick's future? Explain.

Cooperative Learning & Literature
Kagan Publishing • (800) 933-2667 • www.KaganOnline.com

Higher-Level Thinking Cards
Frindle

Directions: Copy enough cards so that each student receives a Question Card. Have students stand up, pair up, and do Traveling Pair Share to respond to each other's questions. Students trade cards and find a new partner to share.

⑨ Frindle

If you had to choose between using the word frindle and getting detention or not using the word and being unpopular, what would you choose and why?

Traveling Pair Share

⑩ Frindle

How can you explain the popularity of the word frindle to your parents?

Traveling Pair Share

⑪ Frindle

What connections can you make between the story and your life? Explain.

Traveling Pair Share

⑫ Frindle

How were Nick's parents supportive during the story? Evaluate their decisions.

Traveling Pair Share

⑬ Frindle

What characteristics does Nick possess? Will these characteristics provide him with the means to be successful as an adult? How?

Traveling Pair Share

⑭ Frindle

What importance did the news article have in helping the word frindle become known around the world?

Traveling Pair Share

⑮ Frindle

What characteristics make a good or bad teacher? How would you describe Mrs. Granger?

Traveling Pair Share

⑯ Frindle

How are words important in our daily lives? Explain.

Traveling Pair Share

Higher-Level Thinking Cards
Frindle

Directions: Copy enough cards so that each student receives a Question Card. Have students stand up, pair up, and do Traveling Pair Share to respond to each other's questions. Students trade cards and find a new partner to share.

---

17 — Frindle

Did Mrs. Granger's predictions come true for Nick?

Traveling Pair Share

---

18 — Frindle

Evaluate the principal's role in the "war of words." Did she help or hinder the war?

Traveling Pair Share

---

19 — Frindle

If you could invent a new word, what would it be and what would it mean? Please describe it to me.

Traveling Pair Share

---

20 — Frindle

Pretend you are Nick and you now have children. They want to know how you became wealthy. What would you say to your children?

Traveling Pair Share

---

21 — Frindle

What symbol would you create for this book? Explain your decision.

Traveling Pair Share

---

22 — Frindle

Could Nick invent a new word for a house object, such as pillow, and make it as successful as the word frindle? Explain.

Traveling Pair Share

---

23 — Frindle

If you wrote the screenplay for this book, would you change any of the story and why?

Traveling Pair Share

---

24 — Frindle

Do you think Nick's parents sided with him to the point it made him spoiled? Explain.

Traveling Pair Share

Cooperative Learning & Literature
Kagan Publishing • (800) 933-2667 • www.KaganOnline.com

Gooney Bird Greene

By Lois Lowry

This story is about an unusually self-confidant girl named Gooney Bird Greene who transferred into Mrs. Pidgeon's 2nd grade class a month after school had started. She likes to be the center of attention, insisting to sit right smack in the center of the classroom, wearing eccentric outfits, and telling outlandish, "absolutely true" stories about how she came from China on a magic carpet ride, her diamond earrings, and how she got her name. She stretches the facts creatively and adds a lot of fun character dialogue and suspense to her stories, which makes everyone in the class want to hear more. The whole class is involved, and not only learns about Gooney Bird Greene, but also how to tell a story.

Reading Level
Lexile Level: 590L
Guided Reading Level: 0
DRA Level: 38
Accelerated Reader: 3.8

Gooney Bird Greene

~ Cooperative Learning Activities ~

Recall Questions
Gooey Bird Greene • Chapters 1–2

❏ **RallyCoach Directions:** Take turns answering each question as your partner coaches. Explain your thinking to your coach.

❏ **Sage-N-Scribe Directions:** The Sage describes what he or she knows about the question so the Scribe can answer the question. The Sage and Scribe switch roles for each question.

Name _____

1. What month did Gooney Bird Greene start school at Watertower Elementary School?
   a. September
   b. October
   c. August
   d. November

2. What did Gooney Bird bring with her to school on her first day?
   a. a yellow polka dotted lunch box
   b. photos from her old school
   c. her book pack filled with special writing paper
   d. her own dictionary

3. What did Mrs. Pidgeon ask her class to think about while she was out of the room?
   a. characters
   b. starting a story
   c. Gooney Bird's name
   d. ways to end a story

4. Why did Gooney Bird want to stand at the front of the classroom to tell her stories?
   a. She wanted everyone to hear her well.
   b. She wanted to see her audience.
   c. She liked to play the teacher.
   d. She wanted to be the center of attention.

5. What type of story does Gooney Bird tell?
   a. made-up stories
   b. stories about her pets
   c. absolutely true stories
   d. stories with lessons

Name _____

1. Where did Gooney Bird Greene live before moving?
   a. Alaska
   b. Australia
   c. China
   d. Europe

2. Why was Malcolm crying during class?
   a. Gooney Bird stuck him with a pencil.
   b. He stuck an origami star up his nose.
   c. He didn't want a new student in class.
   d. His nose started to bleed.

3. What topic did the class want to write about?
   a. Christopher Columbus
   b. Abraham Lincoln
   c. Gooney Bird Greene
   d. Barry Tuckerman

4. What was the subject for Gooney Bird's first story?
   a. her cat
   b. her name
   c. her moving trip
   d. her family

5. How did Gooney Bird come to Watertower?
   a. bus
   b. train
   c. airplane
   d. flying carpet

Recall Questions
Gooney Bird Greene • Chapters 3–4

❑ **RallyCoach Directions:** Take turns answering each question as your partner coaches. Explain your thinking to your coach.

❑ **Sage-N-Scribe Directions:** The Sage describes what he or she knows about the question so the Scribe can answer the question. The Sage and Scribe switch roles for each question.

Name _____

1. **On Friday, what was Mrs. Pidgeon doing when Gooney Bird began telling her story?**
   a. taking notes
   b. grading her oral report
   c. correcting spelling papers
   d. checking her email

2. **What item did Mrs. Greene refuse to leave behind when moving?**
   a. rolled up carpet from the front porch
   b. a vase that has been in the family for years
   c. the family dog
   d. her mother's baking bowl

3. **In what grade was Gooney Bird?**
   a. 3rd grade
   b. 2nd grade
   c. 1st grade
   d. 4th grade

4. **Who is Napoleon?**
   a. Gooney Bird's best friend
   b. an orange and gray cat
   c. a large black poodle
   d. a student in Gooney Bird's class

5. **Where did Gooney Bird Greene get her diamond earrings?**
   a. the supermarket
   b. from her grandmother
   c. the prize in a cereal box
   d. a gumball machine

Name _____

1. **Why did Gooney Bird Greene move to Watertower?**
   a. Her grandmother invited them to live with her.
   b. Her dad got a new job in Watertower.
   c. China was too crowded.
   d. The schools were better in Watertower.

2. **What caused Gooney Bird and Catman to take a flying carpet ride?**
   a. The carpet fell off the roof.
   b. Gooney Bird took a dare.
   c. The car ran over a pot hole.
   d. It was a ride at the amusement park.

3. **What was unique about Gooney Bird's earrings?**
   a. They were purple diamonds.
   b. They were stickers.
   c. They screw into her ears.
   d. They were her grandmother's earrings

4. **Why was the class beginning to get bored?**
   a. Gooney began describing the clothing and didn't have enough suspense.
   b. Mrs. Pidgeon decided to give the class a worksheet to do about characters.
   c. The students had already heard the story.
   d. It started to sound fishy.

5. **The palace was actually…**
   a. a king's home
   b. a toy store
   c. an ice cream shop
   d. an arcade

Cooperative Learning & Literature
Kagan Publishing • (800) 933-2667 • www.KaganOnline.com

Recall Questions
Gooney Bird Greene • Chapters 5–7

❏ **RallyCoach Directions:** Take turns answering each question as your partner coaches. Explain your thinking to your coach.

❏ **Sage-N-Scribe Directions:** The Sage describes what he or she knows about the question so the Scribe can answer the question. The Sage and Scribe switch roles for each question.

Name _____

1. Why was everyone sad on Tuesday?
   a. Mrs. Pidgeon had a substitute.
   b. Malcolm was sick.
   c. Gooney Bird was not in class.
   d. The principal said there were no more stories.

2. What word did Gooney Bird tell students to add to their stories if they get stuck?
   a. suddenly
   b. finally
   c. surprisingly
   d. next

3. What was Gooney Bird Greene's surprise?
   a. She showed the video of the flying carpet report.
   b. She invited her mother to come in to tell a story.
   c. The orchestra came to play a saraband.
   d. She asked all the students to share a story.

4. What caused Gooney Bird to stop for cat-getting-big-suddenly stories?
   a. Mrs. Pidgeon interrupted.
   b. The bell rang.
   c. Barry shouted out about his cat.
   d. Gooney Bird wanted to take a break.

5. Why did Mr. Greene have to pack forty-three sets of false teeth?
   a. He was a special dentist who makes teeth.
   b. He was a denture salesman.
   c. He liked to eat hard candy.
   d. He was going to donate them.

Name _____

1. What was Gooney Bird Greene's excuse for being late?
   a. Her mother's car wouldn't start.
   b. She had to direct an orchestra.
   c. The prince called to take her on a carpet ride.
   d. She overslept and didn't hear the alarm.

2. Why was it a good decision for Gooney Bird to wear long black gloves?
   a. It was very cold outside.
   b. She told a story about her gloves.
   c. The class could see her telling her stories.
   d. Everyone could see her pointing her finger.

3. What does Gooney Bird Greene do before she tells a story?
   a. takes a deep breath
   b. looks at her diary
   c. asks a question
   d. draws a picture

4. Why did Catman stay at the farm?
   a. The cow ate the cat.
   b. The cat was in love with the cow.
   c. The cat liked the farmer.
   d. The farmer's wife gave Catman fresh milk.

5. How did Gooney Bird describe untold stories?
   a. mysteries
   b. interesting
   c. invisible
   d. waiting adventures

Recall Questions
Gooney Bird Greene • End-of-Book

Directions: Participate in Find Someone Who to answer the recall questions about *Gooney Bird Greene*. Write the answer in the space provided. Have your partner initial the answer.

1 Why did Catman stay at the farm?

_____ Initials

2 What three things do all stories need, according to Mrs. Pidgeon?

_____ Initials

3 Where did Gooney Bird direct the orchestra?

_____ Initials

4 Where did Gooney Bird live before Watertower?

_____ Initials

5 What did Mr. Greene pack for the move to Watertower?

_____ Initials

6 What grade was Gooney Bird in during the story?

_____ Initials

7 All of Gooney Bird's stories were absolutely what?

_____ Initials

8 Why did Mrs. Pidgeon have to take Malcolm to the nurse?

_____ Initials

9 Where did Gooney Bird get her diamond earrings?

_____ Initials

10 Why was Gooney Bird Greene interviewed by a reporter?

_____ Initials

11 What did Gooney Bird give the class for dessert?

_____ Initials

12 What is a Laysan Albatross?

_____ Initials

Cooperative Learning & Literature
Kagan Publishing • (800) 933-2667 • www.KaganOnline.com

Higher-Level Thinking Cards
Gooney Bird Greene

Directions: Copy enough cards so that each student receives a Question Card. Have students stand up, pair up, and do Traveling Pair Share to respond to each other's questions. Students trade cards and find a new partner to share.

① **Gooney Bird Greene**

What can you learn from Gooney Bird Greene about writing?

Traveling Pair Share

② **Gooney Bird Greene**

How would you describe Gooney Bird Greene?

Traveling Pair Share

③ **Gooney Bird Greene**

How would you react if a new student came into your class wearing a tutu?

Traveling Pair Share

④ **Gooney Bird Greene**

How does the class change from the beginning of the story to the end?

Traveling Pair Share

⑤ **Gooney Bird Greene**

How does Gooney Bird act like a teacher?

Traveling Pair Share

⑥ **Gooney Bird Greene**

What story would you tell if you were in Gooney Bird's class?

Traveling Pair Share

⑦ **Gooney Bird Greene**

What strategies do you use when telling or writing a story?

Traveling Pair Share

⑧ **Gooney Bird Greene**

How are you like Gooney Bird Greene? Explain.

Traveling Pair Share

Higher-Level Thinking Cards
Gooney Bird Greene

Directions: Copy enough cards so that each student receives a Question Card. Have students stand up, pair up, and do Traveling Pair Share to respond to each other's questions. Students trade cards and find a new partner to share.

⑨ Gooney Bird Greene How are you different from Gooney Bird Greene? Explain. *Traveling Pair Share*	**⑩ Gooney Bird Greene** If you got to choose an outfit like Gooney Bird's, what would you wear and why? *Traveling Pair Share*
⑪ Gooney Bird Greene Does Gooney Bird care about other students' opinions? Why or why not? Explain. *Traveling Pair Share*	**⑫ Gooney Bird Greene** If you could change a part of the story, what would it be and why? *Traveling Pair Share*
⑬ Gooney Bird Greene What would Gooney Bird's next story be? Describe. *Traveling Pair Share*	**⑭ Gooney Bird Greene** How does the teacher react to Gooney Bird's stories? Explain. *Traveling Pair Share*
⑮ Gooney Bird Greene What positive character traits does Gooney Bird show? Please describe them to me. *Traveling Pair Share*	**⑯ Gooney Bird Greene** Imagine you were new to Watertower Elementary. Describe your first day in Mrs. Pidgeon's classroom. *Traveling Pair Share*

Cooperative Learning & Literature
Kagan Publishing • (800) 933-2667 • www.KaganOnline.com

Gregor the Overlander

By Suzanne Collins

Gregor is an 11-year-old boy who lives in New York City with his mother, slightly delusional grandmother, and his little sister, Boots. He is stuck at home babysitting for the summer because his mother works and his dad disappeared 2 years before. Gregor and Boots fall through a grate in the laundry room and land in a place called the Underland, which may have something to do with his father's disappearance. They find themselves among oversized bats, cockroaches, rats, and spiders that take them to a city called Regalia where they learn of the Prophecy of Gray. Gregor and Boots meet other humans and they embark on a quest to find their long-lost father, allying with a specific bat (Ares) and two cockroaches (Tick and Temp). There are many challenges along the way as they encounter the military and the hierarchy social structure of the Underland.

Reading Level
Lexile Level: 630
Guided Reading Level: T
DRA Level: 44–50
Accelerated Reader: 4.8

Gregor the Overlander

~ Cooperative Learning Activities ~

Cooperative Learning & Literature
Kagan Publishing • (800) 933-2667 • www.KaganOnline.com

Character and Description Cards
Gregor the Overlander

Directions: Cut out each card along the dotted line. Matching cards are presented side by side in the book. Give each student one matching card to play Mix-N-Match.

Gregor the Overlander

How would you describe this character?

Gregor

Mix-N-Match

Gregor the Overlander

Which character matches this description?
Considered an Overlander, 11 years old, older brother of Boots, considered a warrior in the Underland.

Mix-N-Match

Gregor the Overlander

How would you describe this character?

Luxa

Mix-N-Match

Gregor the Overlander

Which character matches this description?
Queen of Regalia, bonded to Aurora, seems arrogant to others, stubborn, strong leader.

Mix-N-Match

Gregor the Overlander

How would you describe this character?

Boots

Mix-N-Match

Gregor the Overlander

Which character matches this description?
Also known as Margaret, 2-year-old sister of Gregor, the cockroaches's (or crawlers's) "princess," not fearful.

Mix-N-Match

Gregor the Overlander

How would you describe this character?

Ares

Mix-N-Match

Gregor the Overlander

Which character matches this description?
A bat, bonded to Henry and then later to Gregor, considered a "bad boy" of the bats, strong and powerful.

Mix-N-Match

Character and Description Cards
Gregor the Overlander

Directions: Cut out each card along the dotted line. Matching cards are presented side by side in the book. Give each student one matching card to play Mix-N-Match.

Gregor the Overlander

How would you describe this character?

Aurora

Mix-N-Match

Gregor the Overlander

Which character matches this description?
A bat, golden in color, bonded to Luxa, quiet and shy, doesn't speak often to others besides Luxa.

Mix-N-Match

Gregor the Overlander

How would you describe this character?

Ripred

Mix-N-Match

Gregor the Overlander

Which character matches this description?
A gnawer (rat), friend of Vikus, sharp tongued, gives Gregor a hard time, strong and intelligent fighter, has scar on face, lives on mutual need.

Mix-N-Match

Gregor the Overlander

How would you describe this character?

Vikus

Mix-N-Match

Gregor the Overlander

Which character matches this description?
Luxa's and Henry's grandfather, not in charge of Regalia but works closely with the council to make decisions, believes in peace.

Mix-N-Match

Gregor the Overlander

How would you describe this character?

Solovet

Mix-N-Match

Gregor the Overlander

Which character matches this description?
Luxa's grandmother and married to Vikus, leader of the Regalian army.

Mix-N-Match

Cooperative Learning & Literature
Kagan Publishing • (800) 933-2667 • www.KaganOnline.com

Character and Description Cards
Gregor the Overlander

Directions: Cut out each card along the dotted line. Matching cards are presented side by side in the book. Give each student one matching card to play Mix-N-Match.

Gregor the Overlander
How would you describe this character?
Temp

Gregor the Overlander
Which character matches this description?
A crawler, Boots's best friend in Underland, always with Boots when she is there, runs away from fighting except if Boots is involved, quiet but knowledgeable even though others don't think so.

Gregor the Overlander
How would you describe this character?
Tick

Gregor the Overlander
Which character matches this description?
A crawler, dies on the bridge with the rats to save Boots's life.

Gregor the Overlander
How would you describe this character?
Henry

Gregor the Overlander
Which character matches this description?
Luxa's cousin, found to have joined in with the rats to gain power thus threatening Luxa's life, dies when his bond does not save him and he falls with King Gorger.

Gregor the Overlander
How would you describe this character?
King Gorger

Gregor the Overlander
An evil rat king tries to make everyone follow him, ends up dying by falling off a cliff.

Character Cards
Gregor the Overlander

Directions: Copy the Character Cards for *Gregor the Overlander* by Suzanne Collins, one per student. Cut each card along the dotted line and follow the directions for Who Am I?.

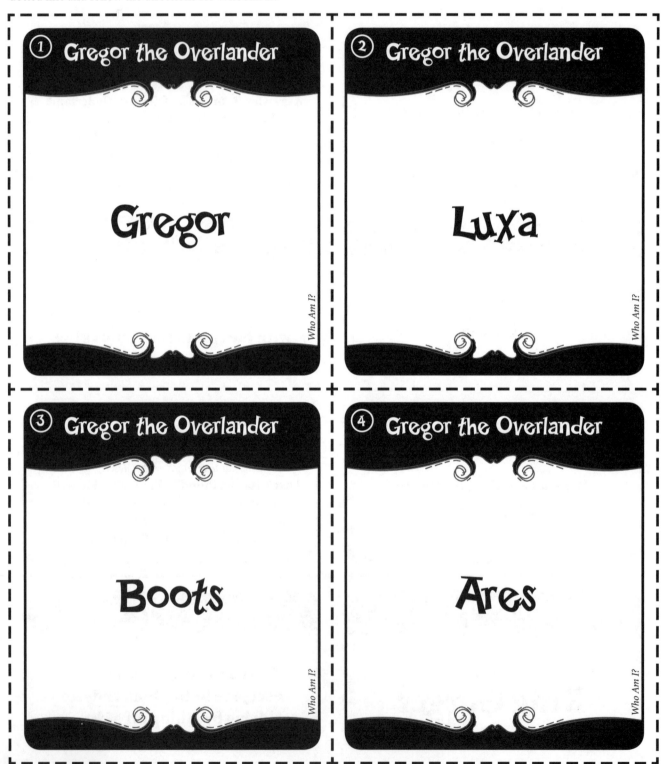

① **Gregor the Overlander**

Gregor

Who Am I?

② **Gregor the Overlander**

Luxa

Who Am I?

③ **Gregor the Overlander**

Boots

Who Am I?

④ **Gregor the Overlander**

Ares

Who Am I?

Cooperative Learning & Literature
Kagan Publishing • (800) 933-2667 • www.KaganOnline.com

Character Cards
Gregor the Overlander

Directions: Copy the Character Cards for *Gregor the Overlander* by Suzanne Collins, one per student. Cut each card along the dotted line and follow the directions for Who Am I?.

⑤ Gregor the Overlander

Aurora

Who Am I?

⑥ Gregor the Overlander

Ripred

Who Am I?

⑦ Gregor the Overlander

Vikus

Who Am I?

⑧ Gregor the Overlander

Solovet

Who Am I?

Character Cards
Gregor the Overlander

Directions: Copy the Character Cards for *Gregor the Overlander* by Suzanne Collins, one per student. Cut each card along the dotted line and follow the directions for Who Am I?.

⑨ Gregor the Overlander	⑩ Gregor the Overlander
Temp	Tick
Who Am I?	*Who Am I?*

⑪ Gregor the Overlander	⑫ Gregor the Overlander
Henry	King Gorger
Who Am I?	*Who Am I?*

Cooperative Learning & Literature
Kagan Publishing • (800) 933-2667 • www.KaganOnline.com

Recall Questions
Gregor the Overlander • Chapters 1–5

Directions: Participate in Find Someone Who to answer the recall questions about *Gregor the Overlander*. Circle the correct answer provided by your partner and have your partner initial the answer.

1 How many gateways open into the Underland?

a. six
b. two
c. one
d. five

_____
Initials

2 What was Gregor's rule to prevent sadness?

a. to stay with his sister Boots all summer
b. to read to his grandmother every night
c. to always stay in the present and not look into the future
d. to never ask adults questions

_____
Initials

3 Who did the cockroaches believe Boots to be?

a. a smelly baby in need of a diaper change
b. a very pretty Overlander
c. a queen or princess
d. Gregor's best friend

_____
Initials

4 How were Gregor and Boots held captive inside the stadium?

a. Bats encircled them.
b. Rats made a wall with tails.
c. The Underlanders blocked the stadium door.
d. Cockroaches came into the stadium.

_____
Initials

5 What thought did Gregor have while taking a bath?

a. That water in the Underland was warmer than at home.
b. The water must lead out of the palace.
c. Boots must be scared that she will never return home.
d. His dad must be in the Underland.

_____
Initials

6 Why was Gregor unable to go to summer camp?

a. His mom couldn't afford to send all her kids to camp.
b. His dad wasn't there to go to camp with him.
c. Gregor didn't want to leave his mom.
d. Gregor had to watch Boots.

_____
Initials

7 How did Boots get the ball from the queen?

a. kicked her in the shin
b. poked her in the eye
c. said, "*Pleeeeeeease!*"
d. ran into her and knocked her down

_____
Initials

8 What did Gregor and Boots see when they first arrived in the Underland?

a. a glittering waterfall
b. darkness and fluttering stars
c. the largest cockroach they had ever seen
d. rats running away into the darkness

_____
Initials

9 What genre is Gregor the Overlander?

a. nonfiction
b. biography
c. fantasy
d. fairy tale

_____
Initials

Recall Questions
Gregor the Overlander • Chapters 6–10

Directions: Participate in Find Someone Who to answer the recall questions about *Gregor the Overlander*. Circle the correct answer provided by your partner and have your partner initial the answer.

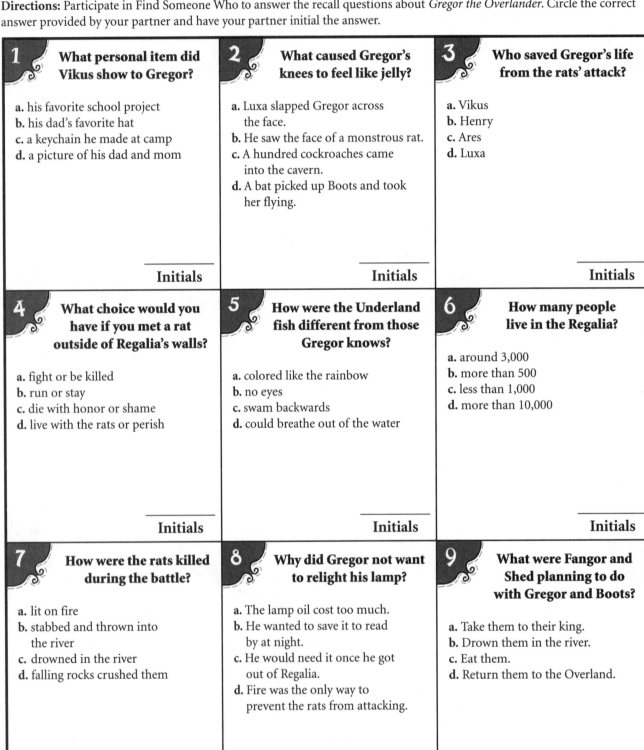

1 What personal item did Vikus show to Gregor?

a. his favorite school project
b. his dad's favorite hat
c. a keychain he made at camp
d. a picture of his dad and mom

Initials

2 What caused Gregor's knees to feel like jelly?

a. Luxa slapped Gregor across the face.
b. He saw the face of a monstrous rat.
c. A hundred cockroaches came into the cavern.
d. A bat picked up Boots and took her flying.

Initials

3 Who saved Gregor's life from the rats' attack?

a. Vikus
b. Henry
c. Ares
d. Luxa

Initials

4 What choice would you have if you met a rat outside of Regalia's walls?

a. fight or be killed
b. run or stay
c. die with honor or shame
d. live with the rats or perish

Initials

5 How were the Underland fish different from those Gregor knows?

a. colored like the rainbow
b. no eyes
c. swam backwards
d. could breathe out of the water

Initials

6 How many people live in the Regalia?

a. around 3,000
b. more than 500
c. less than 1,000
d. more than 10,000

Initials

7 How were the rats killed during the battle?

a. lit on fire
b. stabbed and thrown into the river
c. drowned in the river
d. falling rocks crushed them

Initials

8 Why did Gregor not want to relight his lamp?

a. The lamp oil cost too much.
b. He wanted to save it to read by at night.
c. He would need it once he got out of Regalia.
d. Fire was the only way to prevent the rats from attacking.

Initials

9 What were Fangor and Shed planning to do with Gregor and Boots?

a. Take them to their king.
b. Drown them in the river.
c. Eat them.
d. Return them to the Overland.

Initials

Cooperative Learning & Literature
Kagan Publishing • (800) 933-2667 • www.KaganOnline.com

Recall Questions
Gregor the Overlander • Chapters 11–16

Directions: Participate in Find Someone Who to answer the recall questions about *Gregor the Overlander*. Circle the correct answer provided by your partner and have your partner initial the answer.

1 Why did Gregor take the bottle of root beer from the museum?

a. He knew he would use it as a weapon in battle.
b. It was his father's favorite drink and reminded him of home.
c. It was the only thing that would make Boots take a nap.
d. They could be used to talk with the cockroaches.

_____
Initials

2 Why did Euripedes request Luxa to teach Gregor how to ride?

a. Gregor was bruising him by holding on too tight.
b. Gregor screamed too loud when flying.
c. Euripedes wanted to make sure Gregor knew what to do in battle.
d. Gregor did not know how to guide Euripedes.

_____
Initials

3 Why did Boots put someone into a song?

a. She learned their name.
b. She wanted them to be her friend.
c. She really liked them.
d. She needed them to go to sleep.

_____
Initials

4 Who would be ruler of Regalia at the age of 16?

a. Luxa
b. Henry
c. Gregor
d. Boots

_____
Initials

5 According to the prophecy, how many bats are needed for the quest?

a. three
b. five
c. two
d. four

_____
Initials

6 What creature is known as a spinner in the Underland?

a. cockroach
b. spider
c. rat
d. mole

_____
Initials

7 How did the cockroaches save Gregor and Boots as they ran from the rats?

a. built a wall blocking the tunnel
b. swatted the rats with their tails
c. made a hissing noise
d. dropped spider webs

_____
Initials

8 What was most precious to the Underlanders?

a. their queen
b. fresh water
c. fire
d. light

_____
Initials

9 Who was coming for the Underlanders?

a. spiders
b. cockroaches
c. rats
d. Overlanders

_____
Initials

Recall Questions
Gregor the Overlander • Chapters 17–20

Directions: Participate in Find Someone Who to answer the recall questions about *Gregor the Overlander*. Circle the correct answer provided by your partner and have your partner initial the answer.

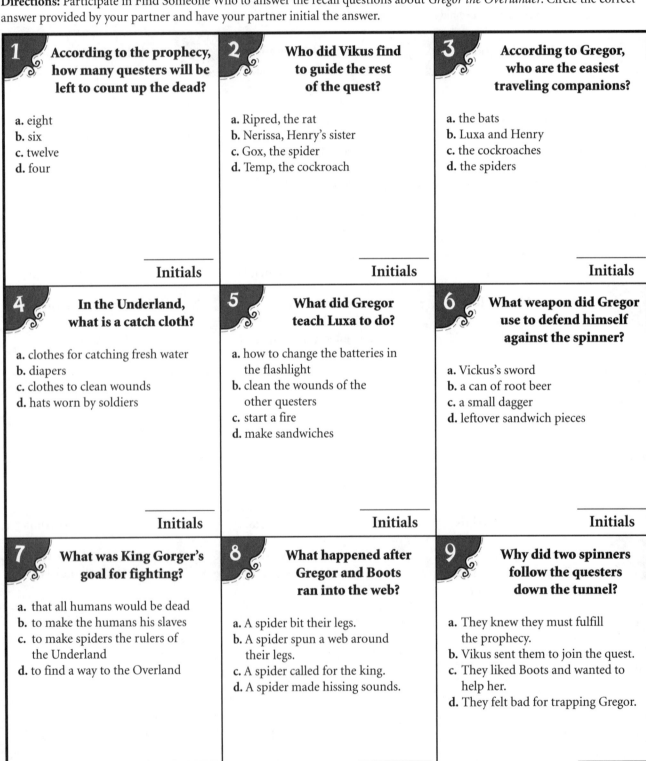

1 According to the prophecy, how many questers will be left to count up the dead?

a. eight
b. six
c. twelve
d. four

Initials

2 Who did Vikus find to guide the rest of the quest?

a. Ripred, the rat
b. Nerissa, Henry's sister
c. Gox, the spider
d. Temp, the cockroach

Initials

3 According to Gregor, who are the easiest traveling companions?

a. the bats
b. Luxa and Henry
c. the cockroaches
d. the spiders

Initials

4 In the Underland, what is a catch cloth?

a. clothes for catching fresh water
b. diapers
c. clothes to clean wounds
d. hats worn by soldiers

Initials

5 What did Gregor teach Luxa to do?

a. how to change the batteries in the flashlight
b. clean the wounds of the other questers
c. start a fire
d. make sandwiches

Initials

6 What weapon did Gregor use to defend himself against the spinner?

a. Vickus's sword
b. a can of root beer
c. a small dagger
d. leftover sandwich pieces

Initials

7 What was King Gorger's goal for fighting?

a. that all humans would be dead
b. to make the humans his slaves
c. to make spiders the rulers of the Underland
d. to find a way to the Overland

Initials

8 What happened after Gregor and Boots ran into the web?

a. A spider bit their legs.
b. A spider spun a web around their legs.
c. A spider called for the king.
d. A spider made hissing sounds.

Initials

9 Why did two spinners follow the questers down the tunnel?

a. They knew they must fulfill the prophecy.
b. Vikus sent them to join the quest.
c. They liked Boots and wanted to help her.
d. They felt bad for trapping Gregor.

Initials

Cooperative Learning & Literature
Kagan Publishing • (800) 933-2667 • www.KaganOnline.com

Recall Questions
Gregor the Overlander • Chapters 21–27

Directions: Participate in Find Someone Who to answer the recall questions about *Gregor the Overlander*. Circle the correct answer provided by your partner and have your partner initial the answer.

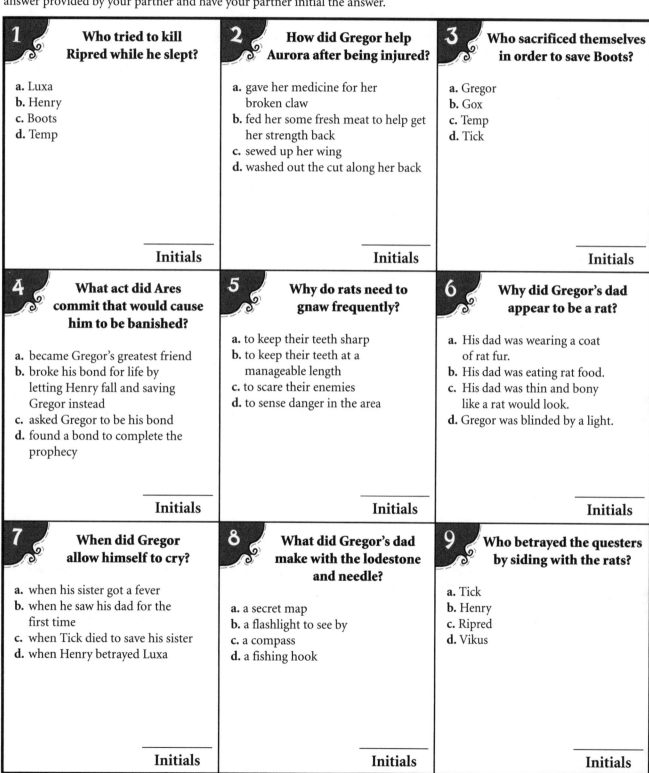

1 Who tried to kill Ripred while he slept?

a. Luxa
b. Henry
c. Boots
d. Temp

_____
Initials

2 How did Gregor help Aurora after being injured?

a. gave her medicine for her broken claw
b. fed her some fresh meat to help get her strength back
c. sewed up her wing
d. washed out the cut along her back

_____
Initials

3 Who sacrificed themselves in order to save Boots?

a. Gregor
b. Gox
c. Temp
d. Tick

_____
Initials

4 What act did Ares commit that would cause him to be banished?

a. became Gregor's greatest friend
b. broke his bond for life by letting Henry fall and saving Gregor instead
c. asked Gregor to be his bond
d. found a bond to complete the prophecy

_____
Initials

5 Why do rats need to gnaw frequently?

a. to keep their teeth sharp
b. to keep their teeth at a manageable length
c. to scare their enemies
d. to sense danger in the area

_____
Initials

6 Why did Gregor's dad appear to be a rat?

a. His dad was wearing a coat of rat fur.
b. His dad was eating rat food.
c. His dad was thin and bony like a rat would look.
d. Gregor was blinded by a light.

_____
Initials

7 When did Gregor allow himself to cry?

a. when his sister got a fever
b. when he saw his dad for the first time
c. when Tick died to save his sister
d. when Henry betrayed Luxa

_____
Initials

8 What did Gregor's dad make with the lodestone and needle?

a. a secret map
b. a flashlight to see by
c. a compass
d. a fishing hook

_____
Initials

9 Who betrayed the questers by siding with the rats?

a. Tick
b. Henry
c. Ripred
d. Vikus

_____
Initials

Recall Questions
Gregor the Overlander • End-of-Book

Directions: Participate in Find Someone Who to answer the recall questions about *Gregor the Overlander*. Circle the correct answer provided by your partner and have your partner initial the answer.

1 Why did Gregor and Boots need to bathe?

a. They needed to be clean before meeting the leader.
b. They wanted to hide.
c. They needed to wash off the smell of the Overland for their protection.
d. They were covered in garbage.

_____ Initials

2 What did the questers use to predict the outcome?

a. the Son of the Sun document
b. the Prophecy of Gray
c. the King's story
d. the Constitution of the Underland

_____ Initials

3 Where did the rats wait so they could ambush the quest?

a. under a ridge
b. the valley
c. by the bridge
d. in the cave

_____ Initials

4 Where did Ripred lead the questers to help disguise their smell?

a. through the river
b. in a dripping tunnel
c. in the air
d. in a carriage

_____ Initials

5 Who was secretly working for the rats?

a. Henry
b. Ripred
c. Vikus
d. Luxa

_____ Initials

6 How many questers would die?

a. only two
b. all of them
c. half of them
d. four

_____ Initials

7 What could Boots do that no one else could do?

a. She understood the language of the spiders.
b. She could tell the difference between the cockroaches.
c. She could sing while she slept.
d. She could see the future.

_____ Initials

8 Who was the leader of the Underlanders until Luxa reached age?

a. Vikus
b. Ripred
c. Henry
d. a cockroach

_____ Initials

9 Who was the first to find Gregor and Boots in the Underland?

a. their dad
b. a cockroach
c. Henry
d. a rat

_____ Initials

10 Who fulfilled the prophecy as warrior?

a. Boots
b. Vikus
c. Henry
d. Gregor

_____ Initials

11 Who did Vikus find to guide the quest?

a. Tick
b. Henry
c. Mareth
d. Ripred

_____ Initials

12 Who developed a fever during the quest?

a. Boots
b. Gregor
c. Henry
d. Tick

_____ Initials

Cooperative Learning & Literature
Kagan Publishing • (800) 933-2667 • www.KaganOnline.com

Journal Writing
Gregor the Overlander • Chapter 5

Directions: Think about the Journal Question, and then write your own response. When done, RoundRobin share your writing with your teammates. Use the space at the bottom to record ideas your teammates share.

Journal Question
How do Gregor and Boots react differently to arriving in the Underland?
Evaluate and explain the differences in how they handle this unexpected event.

Journal Response: _____

_____

_____

_____

_____

_____

_____

_____

_____

_____

_____

_____

_____

Ideas Teammates Shared

Journal Writing
Gregor the Overlander • Chapter 10

Directions: Think about the Journal Question, and then write your own response. When done, RoundRobin share your writing with your teammates. Use the space at the bottom to record ideas your teammates share.

Journal Question
Which group is the most powerful in the Underland? Support your answer using story details.

Journal Response: _____

_____

_____

_____

_____

_____

_____

_____

_____

_____

_____

_____

Ideas Teammates Shared

Cooperative Learning & Literature
Kagan Publishing • (800) 933-2667 • www.KaganOnline.com

Journal Writing
Gregor the Overlander • Chapter 15

Directions: Think about the Journal Question, and then write your own response. When done, RoundRobin share your writing with your teammates. Use the space at the bottom to record ideas your teammates share.

Journal Question
How is Boots important to the development of the story? Explain your answer.

Journal Response: _____

_____

_____

_____

_____

_____

_____

_____

_____

_____

_____

_____

Ideas Teammates Shared

Journal Writing
Gregor the Overlander • End-of-Book

Directions: Think about the Journal Question, and then write your own response. When done, RoundRobin share your writing with your teammates. Use the space at the bottom to record ideas your teammates share.

Journal Question
If you were Gregor, would you choose to stay in the Underland or return home?
Explain and justify your answer.

Journal Response: _____

_____

_____

_____

_____

_____

_____

_____

_____

_____

_____

Ideas Teammates Shared

Cooperative Learning & Literature
Kagan Publishing • (800) 933-2667 • www.KaganOnline.com

Higher-Level Thinking Cards
Gregor the Overlander

Directions: Copy enough cards so that each student receives a Question Card. Have students stand up, pair up, and do Traveling Pair Share to respond to each other's questions. Students trade cards and find a new partner to share.

---

① Gregor the Overlander

How does Gregor change from the beginning of the story to the end?

Traveling Pair Share

---

② Gregor the Overlander

How are Gregor and Luxa alike? Different?

Traveling Pair Share

---

③ Gregor the Overlander

How have the people of the Underland adapted to living in Regalia?

Traveling Pair Share

---

④ Gregor the Overlander

What character traits make a hero? Is Gregor a hero? Explain.

Traveling Pair Share

---

⑤ Gregor the Overlander

How has losing his father affected Gregor throughout the story?

Traveling Pair Share

---

⑥ Gregor the Overlander

How would the story be different if Gregor had not jumped off the cliff at the end of the story?

Traveling Pair Share

---

⑦ Gregor the Overlander

What conclusions can you make about Ripred's life? Explain.

Traveling Pair Share

---

⑧ Gregor the Overlander

Which group (crawlers, gnawers, spinners, Regalians) do you think has the most power in the Underland? Explain.

Traveling Pair Share

Higher-Level Thinking Cards
Gregor the Overlander

Directions: Copy enough cards so that each student receives a Question Card. Have students stand up, pair up, and do Traveling Pair Share to respond to each other's questions. Students trade cards and find a new partner to share.

---

⑨ Gregor the Overlander

Do you think the Prophecy of Gray predicted the quest's outcome or did the questers make the prophecy come true?

Traveling Pair Share

---

⑩ Gregor the Overlander

What preparations would you have made if you were in Gregor's position before fighting the rats?

Traveling Pair Share

---

⑪ Gregor the Overlander

How will Gregor be different in the Overland after spending time in the Underland?

Traveling Pair Share

---

⑫ Gregor the Overlander

What is more important, protecting a whole city or your family? Explain.

Traveling Pair Share

---

⑬ Gregor the Overlander

What examples of foreshadowing did the author use to hint at Henry's betrayal?

Traveling Pair Share

---

⑭ Gregor the Overlander

How will Ares be treated after Gregor leaves? What makes you think this?

Traveling Pair Share

---

⑮ Gregor the Overlander

What importance does Boots play in the story? How would it have been different if Gregor did not take her on the quest?

Traveling Pair Share

---

⑯ Gregor the Overlander

What importance do the bats play to the Regalians's way of survival?

Traveling Pair Share

Cooperative Learning & Literature
Kagan Publishing • (800) 933-2667 • www.KaganOnline.com

Higher-Level Thinking Cards
Gregor *the* Overlander

Directions: Copy enough cards so that each student receives a Question Card. Have students stand up, pair up, and do Traveling Pair Share to respond to each other's questions. Students trade cards and find a new partner to share.

---

17 — Gregor *the* Overlander

Do you agree or disagree with Gregor's decision to bond with Ares? Explain?

Traveling Pair Share

---

18 — Gregor *the* Overlander

Does this story remind you of another story you have read? Explain.

Traveling Pair Share

---

19 — Gregor *the* Overlander

Are you more like Gregor or Luxa? What in the story makes you think this?

Traveling Pair Share

---

20 — Gregor *the* Overlander

How does Gregor's relationship with Luxa change over the course of the story?

Traveling Pair Share

---

21 — Gregor *the* Overlander

Describe Vikus's relationship with his granddaughter, Luxa. What conclusions can you make?

Traveling Pair Share

---

22 — Gregor *the* Overlander

If you could ask Ripred a question, what would it be and why?

Traveling Pair Share

---

23 — Gregor *the* Overlander

Describe how Henry and Luxa reacted to Ripred joining the quest. Was this reaction justified?

Traveling Pair Share

---

24 — Gregor *the* Overlander

What will Gregor, Boots, and their dad tell their mom when they return home? Will she believe them? Why or why not?

Traveling Pair Share

Higher-Level Thinking Cards
Gregor the Overlander

Directions: Copy enough cards so that each student receives a Question Card. Have students stand up, pair up, and do Traveling Pair Share to respond to each other's questions. Students trade cards and find a new partner to share.

---

25 Gregor the Overlander

Will Gregor return to Regalia? Explain your reasoning.

Traveling Pair Share

---

26 Gregor the Overlander

What do you think Mom had been doing during the time Gregor and Boots were away?

Traveling Pair Share

---

27 Gregor the Overlander

How is Regalia like the world we live in? How is it different?

Traveling Pair Share

---

28 Gregor the Overlander

After reading this book, what advice would you give Gregor or Luxa before going on the quest?

Traveling Pair Share

---

29 Gregor the Overlander

How do you think Luxa would react if she found herself in the Overland?

Traveling Pair Share

---

30 Gregor the Overlander

If you could retitle the book, what would you title it? Explain.

Traveling Pair Share

---

31 Gregor the Overlander

How have the rats, crawlers, and bats adapted to living in Regalia?

Traveling Pair Share

---

32 Gregor the Overlander

Who else besides Gregor is a hero in the story? Explain.

Traveling Pair Share

Cooperative Learning & Literature
Kagan Publishing • (800) 933-2667 • www.KaganOnline.com

Henry and Ribsy

By Beverly Cleary

Henry is out of school for the summer and is looking for something to do to keep from being bored. He has a dog named Ribsy who constantly runs into trouble, which could become a problem. Henry makes a deal with his father to keep Ribsy out of trouble in exchange for going on a salmon fishing trip in September. Henry finds this task is harder than he thought when Ribsy tangles with the police, the garbage man, and even Ramona Quimby of the neighborhood.

Reading Level
Lexile Level: 740L
Guided Reading Level: O
DRA Level: 38
Accelerated Reader: 4.6

Henry and Ribsy

~ Cooperative Learning Activities ~

Cooperative Learning & Literature
Kagan Publishing • (800) 933-2667 • www.KaganOnline.com

Recall Questions
Henry and Ribsy • Chapter 1

❏ **RallyCoach Directions:** Take turns answering each question as your partner coaches. Explain your thinking to your coach.

❏ **Sage-N-Scribe Directions:** The Sage describes what he or she knows about the question so the Scribe can answer the question. The Sage and Scribe switch roles for each question.

Name _____

1. What was Ribsy doing when he ran across Mrs. Green's lawn?
   a. looking for a hidden bone
   b. chasing the Grumbies' cat
   c. playing fetch with Henry
   d. running after a lost ball

2. What did Ribsy do while Henry was in the car?
   a. barked at the store robber
   b. chewed on Al's wrench
   c. used the potted plants as a restroom
   d. ate a police officer's sandwich

3. What did Henry have to do in order to go salmon fishing with his dad?
   a. take the garbage out every day
   b. keep Ribsy out of trouble for the next month
   c. get good grades on his report card
   d. train Ribsy to stay put when asked

Name _____

1. What did Henry ask Al at the filling station?
   a. "*How much money do you make?*"
   b. "*Can I help you change the oil?*"
   c. "*Can I ride up on the grease rack?*"
   d. "*May Ribsy stay and watch you work?*"

2. Why did the officer stop at the supermarket?
   a. He wanted some milk to go with his lunch.
   b. A call came in about some kids stealing candy.
   c. He needed to get gas in his car.
   d. It was part of his regular route.

3. What does Henry feed Ribsy?
   a. dry dog food
   b. hot dogs
   c. lunch meat
   d. Woofies

Recall Questions
Henry and Ribsy • Chapter 2

❑ **RallyCoach Directions:** Take turns answering each question as your partner coaches. Explain your thinking to your coach.

❑ **Sage-N-Scribe Directions:** The Sage describes what he or she knows about the question so the Scribe can answer the question. The Sage and Scribe switch roles for each question.

Name _____

1. What would Henry get for taking out the garbage every day?
   a. to go on the fishing trip
   b. 15 cents extra a week in his allowance
   c. going to bed 15 minutes later every night
   d. extra time to watch TV

2. What would cause a dog to be sent to the pound according to Henry?
   a. biting someone
   b. barking nonstop through the night
   c. chasing the neighbor's cat
   d. eating from the neighborhood's garbage cans

3. How did Henry know Ribsy was not a vicious dog?
   a. Ribsy licked Henry's hand.
   b. Ramona was pulling at Ribsy's tail.
   c. Beezus said he was a good dog.
   d. Scooter was able to pet Ribsy.

4. What was Ribsy's reason for growling at Scooter?
   a. Scooter was teasing Henry.
   b. Scooter had taken Ribsy's bone.
   c. Henry told Ribsy to protect him.
   d. Scooter took Henry's bike out of the garage.

Name _____

1. How did Ribsy react to the garbage being picked up?
   a. barked at the window
   b. smelled the garbage man's shoes
   c. growled deep at the garbage man
   d. tugged on Henry's rope

2. Why did the Hugginses have to shut the dining room window?
   a. The garbage smelled bad.
   b. Ribsy kept barking.
   c. Someone was mowing the grass.
   d. Scooter was playing basketball outside.

3. What conclusion did the children make about Ribsy?
   a. He wanted to protect his bone.
   b. He was being a protective watchdog.
   c. He liked Ramona.
   d. He didn't like garbagemen.

4. What deal did Mr. Huggins make with Henry about the garbage?
   a. Henry would still take the garbage out but lock up Ribsy.
   b. Mrs. Huggins would take out the garbage if Henry clipped around the edge of the lawn.
   c. Mrs. Huggins would add 25 cents to Henry's allowance.
   d. Henry would no longer need to do chores.

Cooperative Learning & Literature
Kagan Publishing • (800) 933-2667 • www.KaganOnline.com

Recall Questions
Henry and Ribsy • Chapter 3

❑ **RallyCoach Directions:** Take turns answering each question as your partner coaches. Explain your thinking to your coach.

❑ **Sage-N-Scribe Directions:** The Sage describes what he or she knows about the question so the Scribe can answer the question. The Sage and Scribe switch roles for each question.

Name _____

1. **What did Henry's mom buy at Colossal Drugstore?**
   a. hair dye
   b. shampoo
   c. electric clippers
   d. stylist scissors

2. **What was Henry's solution to his problem in this chapter?**
   a. shave all his hair off
   b. go to the barber to have it fixed
   c. dye his hair a strange color
   d. wear a sailor's hat

3. **What was Ramona doing while Beezus talked with Henry?**
   a. playing fetch with Ribsy
   b. digging holes in the flower bed
   c. eating a pound of butter
   d. pulling on Ribsy's ears

Name _____

1. **Which phrase best describes Henry's feelings about his parents cuttings his hair?**
   a. embarrassed by the chewed up look of the haircut
   b. angry that they didn't let him do it himself
   c. excited that the family is saving money
   d. glad he wasn't the only one with a bad cut

2. **How did Henry distract his friends from talking about his hair?**
   a. brainstorm ways to pull his teeth
   b. show them Ribsy's latest tricks
   c. tell them a joke he heard at camp
   d. tell the story about his mom's attempt to cook

3. **Why would tying a rocket to Henry's loose teeth not work, according to Mary Jane?**
   a. It would hurt.
   b. It was past the Fourth of July.
   c. They wouldn't be able to find a rocket.
   d. Henry refused to try it.

Recall Questions
Henry and Ribsy • Chapter 4

❐ **RallyCoach Directions:** Take turns answering each question as your partner coaches. Explain your thinking to your coach.

❐ **Sage-N-Scribe Directions:** The Sage describes what he or she knows about the question so the Scribe can answer the question. The Sage and Scribe switch roles for each question.

Name _____

1. **Why did Mrs. Huggins tell Henry to stop flapping his teeth?**
   a. He kept talking with his mouth full of food.
   b. He kept wiggling his teeth with his tongue.
   c. He had his fingers in his mouth playing with his teeth.
   d. He was wearing fake teeth to hide his loose teeth.

2. **What was Henry's first thought about why Scooter and Robert were wearing sailor hats?**
   a. They wanted to be popular like him.
   b. They got bad hair cuts as well.
   c. They were making fun of him.
   d. They were going to go salmon fishing.

3. **How did Henry pull his loose teeth out?**
   a. tied a string to his teeth and had Ribsy pull on the rope attached to the string
   b. let Scooter pull them out
   c. tied a string to one tooth and a rock to the other then dropped the rock in the river
   d. tied one end of the string to his teeth and the other end to Robert's bike

Name _____

1. **Why did the price of teeth go from a dime to a quarter per tooth?**
   a. The cost of living has gone up.
   b. Henry requested more money.
   c. No dimes were left.
   d. It cost more to go to the dentist.

2. **What was the real reason Robert and Scooter were wearing the sailor hats?**
   a. They wanted to be popular like him.
   b. They got bad haircuts as well.
   c. They were making fun of him.
   d. They were going to go salmon fishing.

3. **What was Henry able to do once his teeth were pulled?**
   a. eat an apple
   b. spit double
   c. whistle a tune
   d. sip soda through a straw

Cooperative Learning & Literature
Kagan Publishing • (800) 933-2667 • www.KaganOnline.com

Recall Questions
Henry and Ribsy • Chapter 5

❏ **RallyCoach Directions:** Take turns answering each question as your partner coaches. Explain your thinking to your coach.

❏ **Sage-N-Scribe Directions:** The Sage describes what he or she knows about the question so the Scribe can answer the question. The Sage and Scribe switch roles for each question.

Name _____

1. Why was Henry's mother not home when he got back from school?
 a. She was at the PTA meeting.
 b. She was working late.
 c. She went to the store to get food.
 d. She had to pick up clothes at the cleaners.

2. Why was Ramona carrying a lunch box?
 a. She had her sandwich in there.
 b. She was pretending it was a camera.
 c. She was collecting rocks during their walk.
 d. She had her ice cream cone in it.

3. Why was Ribsy following Ramona down the street?
 a. She took his bone.
 b. He wanted more ice cream.
 c. Ramona had taken his ball.
 d. Ramona smelled like horse meat.

4. Why did Mrs. Wisser think Ramona was on the jungle gym?
 a. Ramona was playing.
 b. Ramona was terrified of Ribsy.
 c. Ramona was hiding Ribsy's bone.
 d. Ramona was throwing a tantrum.

Name _____

1. Why did Ramona and Beezus come to Henry's house?
 a. They brought him an ice cream cone.
 b. Beezus wanted to give Henry his homework.
 c. Beezus invited Henry to play checkers.
 d. Henry asked if they wanted go for a bike ride.

2. What did Ribsy do when Ramona and Beezus visited?
 a. hid under the bed
 b. growled at Ramona
 c. ate Ramona's ice cream
 d. licked Beezus's leg

3. Why did Ramona want PTA?
 a. She was hungry.
 b. She wanted her mom at the meeting.
 c. She thought Henry and Beezus were spelling something she couldn't have.
 d. She thought Henry and Beezus were hiding her sandwich.

4. What caused Ramona to finally come down from the jungle gym?
 a. She got her PTA.
 b. Ramona's mom climbed up and got her.
 c. Miss Mullen told her to get down.
 d. Ribsy was taken away by Henry.

Recall Questions
Henry and Ribsy • Chapter 6

❏ **RallyCoach Directions:** Take turns answering each question as your partner coaches. Explain your thinking to your coach.

❏ **Sage-N-Scribe Directions:** The Sage describes what he or she knows about the question so the Scribe can answer the question. The Sage and Scribe switch roles for each question.

Name _____

1. **How did Henry know his father was getting ready to go fishing?**
   a. He was gathering his fishing lures.
   b. He looked up fishing reports on the computer.
   c. He was looking for his tin pants.
   d. He asked Mrs. Huggins to fix him lunch for tomorrow.

2. **Who did Henry and Mr. Huggins go fishing with?**
   a. Mr. Grumbie
   b. Mr. Green
   c. Scooter and his father
   d. Mike

3. **What was the weather like during Henry's fishing trip?**
   a. hot and sunny
   b. chilly and rainy
   c. sunny and rainy
   d. windy and hot

4. **How did Henry get Ribsy back?**
   a. Another fisherman fished him out of the water.
   b. Mr. Huggins pulled him back into the boat.
   c. Henry reached out for him.
   d. Ribsy found Henry when they returned to the boathouse.

Name _____

1. **Why did Ribsy get to go fishing?**
   a. He was good for one month.
   b. He helped Henry with the trash.
   c. Mom said she was on vacation.
   d. Mr. Huggins knew Ribsy would help catch salmon.

2. **What suggestion did Mr. Huggins give Henry about fishing?**
   a. cast his line out as far as he could
   b. don't let Ribsy smell the tackle
   c. drop his line overboard and let it be carried out
   d. be patient and he will catch a fish

3. **What happened when Ribsy saw the salmon?**
   a. He jumped over the side of the boat.
   b. He growled at Mr. Grumbie.
   c. He bit the fish.
   d. He threw it overboard with his tail.

4. **What did Henry know after Mr. Huggins suggested Henry and Ribsy go to the boathouse?**
   a. He was never going to go fishing again.
   b. Mr. Grumbie would not catch another fish.
   c. His chance to catch a salmon was gone.
   d. Ribsy would be grounded for a month.

Cooperative Learning & Literature
Kagan Publishing • (800) 933-2667 • www.KaganOnline.com

Recall Questions
Henry and Ribsy • Chapter 7

❏ **RallyCoach Directions:** Take turns answering each question as your partner coaches. Explain your thinking to your coach.

❏ **Sage-N-Scribe Directions:** The Sage describes what he or she knows about the question so the Scribe can answer the question. The Sage and Scribe switch roles for each question.

Name _____

1. Why did Henry decide to take Ribsy down to the beach?
a. People were making comments about a smelly dog.
b. Henry knew that Ribsy needed to run off energy.
c. He was barking at all the customers.
d. Henry wanted to warm up in the warm sun.

2. What did Ribsy find that excited Henry?
a. a jellyfish
b. a salmon
c. a starfish
d. seashells

3. Why did Henry want to carry the fish as they neared the boathouse?
a. He wanted everyone to know it was his fish.
b. He didn't want the man to take it.
c. He was afraid it would get away.
d. He was cold and shivering.

4. How did Scooter most likely feel about Henry catching a fish?
a. angry that Henry caught a fish and he didn't
b. confused that Henry caught a fish bare-handed
c. embarrassed that he fell in the water
d. excited that Henry caught such a small fish

Name _____

1. What did Henry see when looking through the telescope?
a. Mr. Huggins catch a huge salmon
b. Mr. Grumbie talking with his father about the lost salmon
c. Scooter fishing with his dad
d. Ribsy running down the beach

2. How was Henry finally able to catch a fish?
a. He went out in the boat with Scooter.
b. He borrowed a pole from Mike at the boathouse.
c. He found one laying on the beach.
d. He tackled the fish with his bare hands.

3. How much did Henry's salmon weigh?
a. 30 pounds
b. 25 pounds
c. 29 pounds
d. 33 pounds

4. Why did Henry say, "Good old Ribsy," as he headed to the car?
a. Ribsy protected Henry from Scooter's teasing.
b. Risby had fun fishing in the boat.
c. Ribsy had found Henry when he fell in the water.
d. Ribsy found the salmon Henry caught.

Recall Questions
Henry and Ribsy • End-of-Book

Directions: Participate in Find Someone Who to answer the recall questions about *Henry and Ribsy*. Write the answer in the space provided. Have your partner initial the answer.

1 What happened when the garbage man tried to pick up the Higginses' trash?

_____
_____
_____
_____
Initials

2 Who found the salmon in the shallow water by the beach?

_____
_____
_____
_____
Initials

3 What did Henry want to catch when he went fishing with his dad?

_____
_____
_____
_____
Initials

4 How was Henry finally able to catch a fish?

_____
_____
_____
_____
Initials

5 What did Henry ask to do at Al's Thrifty Service Station?

_____
_____
_____
_____
Initials

6 Who was the one that pulled out Henry's loose teeth?

_____
_____
_____
_____
Initials

7 How did Henry try to hide his bad hair cut?

_____
_____
_____
_____
Initials

8 What happened when Ribsy saw Mr. Grumbie's fish?

_____
_____
_____
_____
Initials

9 What did Henry have to do in order to go salmon fishing in September?

_____
_____
_____
_____
Initials

10 What was Ribsy's reason for following Ramona?

_____
_____
_____
_____
Initials

11 What conclusion did the students make about Ribsy growling at Scooter?

_____
_____
_____
_____
Initials

12 What did Mrs. Huggins purchase at the Colossal Drugstore?

_____
_____
_____
_____
Initials

Cooperative Learning & Literature
Kagan Publishing • (800) 933-2667 • www.KaganOnline.com

Journal Writing
Henry and Ribsy • Chapter 1

Directions: Think about the Journal Question, and then write your own response. When done, RoundRobin share your writing with your teammates. Use the space at the bottom to record ideas your teammates share.

Journal Question
In this chapter, Ribsy ends up eating a police officer's sandwich. How could Henry have prevented this from happening? Explain using story details.

Journal Response: _____

_____

_____

_____

_____

_____

_____

_____

_____

_____

_____

Ideas Teammates Shared

Journal Writing
Henry and Ribsy • Chapter 2

Directions: Think about the Journal Question, and then write your own response. When done, RoundRobin share your writing with your teammates. Use the space at the bottom to record ideas your teammates share.

Journal Question
Why was Ribsy protecting the garbage? What could Henry do to prevent this from happening in the future? Explain.

Journal Response: _____

_____

_____

_____

_____

_____

_____

_____

_____

_____

_____

_____

_____

Ideas Teammates Shared

Cooperative Learning & Literature
Kagan Publishing • (800) 933-2667 • www.KaganOnline.com

Journal Writing
Henry and Ribsy • Chapter 3

Directions: Think about the Journal Question, and then write your own response. When done, RoundRobin share your writing with your teammates. Use the space at the bottom to record ideas your teammates share.

Journal Question
Was it a good or bad decision for Mrs. Huggins to try to cut Henry's hair? Explain.
Have you ever had an experience like Henry's haircut? If so, please explain.

Journal Response: _____

_____

_____

_____

_____

_____

_____

_____

_____

_____

_____

Ideas Teammates Shared

Journal Writing
Henry and Ribsy • Chapter 4

Directions: Think about the Journal Question, and then write your own response. When done, RoundRobin share your writing with your teammates. Use the space at the bottom to record ideas your teammates share.

Journal Question
Ribsy pulls Henry's tooth using his tug rope. Have you ever pulled your tooth in an interesting way? Describe a way you would pull your tooth.

Journal Response: _____

_____

_____

_____

_____

_____

_____

_____

_____

_____

_____

_____

_____

Ideas Teammates Shared

Cooperative Learning & Literature
Kagan Publishing • (800) 933-2667 • www.KaganOnline.com

Journal Writing
Henry and Ribsy • Chapter 5

Directions: Think about the Journal Question, and then write your own response. When done, RoundRobin share your writing with your teammates. Use the space at the bottom to record ideas your teammates share.

Journal Question
How did the moms react to Ramona being on top of the jungle gym?
Was this reaction justified? Explain.

Journal Response: _____

_____

_____

_____

_____

_____

_____

_____

_____

_____

_____

_____

_____

Ideas Teammates Shared

Journal Writing
Henry and Ribsy • Chapter 6

Directions: Think about the Journal Question, and then write your own response. When done, RoundRobin share your writing with your teammates. Use the space at the bottom to record ideas your teammates share.

Journal Question
How do Henry's feelings change throughout his fishing trip? Describe these changes.

Journal Response: _____

_____

_____

_____

_____

_____

_____

_____

_____

_____

_____

Ideas Teammates Shared

Cooperative Learning & Literature
Kagan Publishing • (800) 933-2667 • www.KaganOnline.com

Journal Writing
Henry and Ribsy • Chapter 7

Directions: Think about the Journal Question, and then write your own response. When done, RoundRobin share your writing with your teammates. Use the space at the bottom to record ideas your teammates share.

Journal Question
Pretend you are Henry and you are back at school. How would you tell the story about catching the salmon? Write it below.

Journal Response: _____

_____

_____

_____

_____

_____

_____

_____

_____

_____

_____

Ideas Teammates Shared

Higher-Level Thinking Cards
Henry and Ribsy

Directions: Copy enough cards so that each student receives a Question Card. Have students stand up, pair up, and do Traveling Pair Share to respond to each other's questions. Students trade cards and find a new partner to share.

---

① Henry and Ribsy

In the story, Henry gets a really bad haircut and is worried about going to school. Has anything like this happened to you? Explain.

Traveling Pair Share

---

② Henry and Ribsy

Describe Henry and Ribsy's friendship.

Traveling Pair Share

---

③ Henry and Ribsy

Beverly Cleary has written numerous books. Have you read any of her other books? Please tell me about it. If not, which of her books would you like to read?

Traveling Pair Share

---

④ Henry and Ribsy

What genre of story is *Henry and Ribsy*? Explain.

Traveling Pair Share

---

⑤ Henry and Ribsy

Henry agrees to take out the trash every day for a 15-cent raise in his allowance. Is this a fair or unfair deal? Explain.

Traveling Pair Share

---

⑥ Henry and Ribsy

Mr. Huggins agrees to take Henry fishing if Henry can keep Ribsy out of trouble for a month. Was this a good or bad agreement? Explain.

Traveling Pair Share

---

⑦ Henry and Ribsy

The moms at the PTA meeting were upset that Ribsy had chased Ramona up the jungle gym. Why did they make that conclusion? Was this conclusion justified?

Traveling Pair Share

---

⑧ Henry and Ribsy

If you could do anything with your dad, what would it be and why?

Traveling Pair Share

Cooperative Learning & Literature
Kagan Publishing • (800) 933-2667 • www.KaganOnline.com

Higher-Level Thinking Cards
Henry and Ribsy

Directions: Copy enough cards so that each student receives a Question Card. Have students stand up, pair up, and do Traveling Pair Share to respond to each other's questions. Students trade cards and find a new partner to share.

9 — Henry and Ribsy
If you saw Ribsy growl at the garbageman, would you be afraid? Explain.

10 — Henry and Ribsy
Henry was responsible for taking out the trash. What responsibilities do you have at home?

11 — Henry and Ribsy
What changes did Henry have to make in his routine in order to go fishing?

12 — Henry and Ribsy
How did Henry feel once he was finally able to catch the Chinook?

13 — Henry and Ribsy
What lesson can you learn after reading *Henry and Ribsy*? Explain.

14 — Henry and Ribsy
How does Ribsy affect the neighborhood? Explain.

15 — Henry and Ribsy
Evaluate the PTA moms' reactions after seeing Ramona on top of the jungle gym.

16 — Henry and Ribsy
What do you know about taking care of a dog? Explain it to me.

Higher-Level Thinking Cards
Henry and Ribsy

Directions: Copy enough cards so that each student receives a Question Card. Have students stand up, pair up, and do Traveling Pair Share to respond to each other's questions. Students trade cards and find a new partner to share.

17 Henry and Ribsy
What would have happened if Ribsy didn't jump out of the boat? How would the story be different?
Traveling Pair Share

18 Henry and Ribsy
Why is the fishing trip important to Henry? Explain.
Traveling Pair Share

19 Henry and Ribsy
How do you think the boys at school will react to Henry's story of catching the Chinook? Explain your prediction.
Traveling Pair Share

20 Henry and Ribsy
What is your favorite part of *Henry and Ribsy*? Explain.
Traveling Pair Share

21 Henry and Ribsy
How would you feel if you were Henry right after he caught the fish? Describe your feelings.
Traveling Pair Share

22 Henry and Ribsy
How would the story be different if Ribsy was a cat rather than a dog? Explain.
Traveling Pair Share

23 Henry and Ribsy
Why was Henry trying to think up things to do for the summer? Do you have similar thoughts? Explain.
Traveling Pair Share

24 Henry and Ribsy
Why didn't Miss Mullens call the pound when Ribsy chased Ramona up the jungle gym? Explain.
Traveling Pair Share

Cooperative Learning & Literature
Kagan Publishing • (800) 933-2667 • www.KaganOnline.com

Little House in the Big Woods

By Laura Ingalls Wilder

It is the 1860s and the Ingalls family live in the woods of Wisconsin where their day-to-day life is filled with hardships of prairie life, farming, harvesting crops, hunting for food, trading, cheese-making, maple-sugaring, butter-churning, clothes-making, and craft-making. Ma Ingalls has a way of making the chores fun, so Laura and big sister Mary gladly do what they are told. Laura says baby sister Carrie is the "prettiest baby in the world." The girls have the most fun with Pa when he roughhouses, jokes, plays the fiddle for them, and tells them stories. The stories are the best, but they have many fun times together when playing with cousins, watching the big girls dress up for a dance, and when grandma and grandpa dance the jig. This is a heartwarming story of the unique ways the Ingalls family has fun, shares love, and band together to make the best out of difficult situations.

Reading Level
Lexile Level: 930L
Guided Reading Level: Q
DRA Level: 40
Accelerated Reader: 4.2

Little House in the Big Woods

～ Cooperative Learning Activities ～

Character and Description Cards
Little House in the Big Woods

Directions: Cut out each card along the dotted line. Matching cards are presented side by side in the book. Give each student one matching card to play Mix-N-Match.

Little House in the Big Woods

How would you describe this character?
Laura Ingalls

Little House in the Big Woods

Which character matches this description?
Main character in the book, middle daughter of the Ingalls, likes to climb trees and hear stories from Pa.

Little House in the Big Woods

How would you describe this character?
Ma (Charlotte) Ingalls

Little House in the Big Woods

Which character matches this description?
Laura's mother, considered to be fashionable, does the daily chores at the log cabin, slaps a bear.

Little House in the Big Woods

How would you describe this character?
Pa (Charles) Ingalls

Little House in the Big Woods

Which character matches this description?
Father of Laura, Mary, and baby Carrie; hard worker, sells furs in town, plays fiddle and tells stories to the girls.

Little House in the Big Woods

How would you describe this character?
Mary Ingalls

Little House in the Big Woods

Which character matches this description?
Oldest daughter of the Ingalls, often acts like a mother and helper to her younger sisters, loves to play with dolls.

Character and Description Cards
Little House in the Big Woods

Directions: Cut out each card along the dotted line. Matching cards are presented side by side in the book. Give each student one matching card to play Mix-N-Match.

Little House in the Big Woods

How would you describe this character?
Charley

Mix-N-Match

Little House in the Big Woods

Which character matches this description?
Cousin of Laura and Mary, often causes trouble, spoiled, gets stung by bees.

Mix-N-Match

Little House in the Big Woods

How would you describe this character?
Grandpa Ingalls

Mix-N-Match

Little House in the Big Woods

Which character matches this description?
Father of Pa, gathers sap from the trees, has a dance at his house.

Mix-N-Match

Little House in the Big Woods

How would you describe this character?
Grandma Ingalls

Mix-N-Match

Little House in the Big Woods

Which character matches this description?
Mother of Pa, helps make the maple sugar, very good dancer.

Mix-N-Match

Little House in the Big Woods

How would you describe this character?
Uncle Henry

Mix-N-Match

Little House in the Big Woods

Which character matches this description?
Brother of Charles, father of Charley, helps with the harvest.

Mix-N-Match

Cooperative Learning & Literature
Kagan Publishing • (800) 933-2667 • www.KaganOnline.com

Character and Description Cards
Little House in the Big Woods

Directions: Cut out each card along the dotted line. Matching cards are presented side by side in the book. Give each student one matching card to play Mix-N-Match.

Little House in the Big Woods

How would you describe this character?
Aunt Polly

Mix-N-Match

Little House in the Big Woods

Which character matches this description?
Mom of Charley and sister-in-law of the Ingalls. She used mud to help heal Charley's bee stings.

Mix-N-Match

Little House in the Big Woods

How would you describe this character?
Baby Carrie

Mix-N-Match

Little House in the Big Woods

Which character matches this description?
Youngest daughter of the Ingalls, often cared for by her older sisters.

Mix-N-Match

Little House in the Big Woods

How would you describe this character?
Jack

Mix-N-Match

Little House in the Big Woods

Which character matches this description?
Loyal dog of the Ingalls that proves to be very loyal and protective of the Ingalls.

Mix-N-Match

Little House in the Big Woods

How would you describe this character?
Aunt Lotty

Mix-N-Match

Little House in the Big Woods

Which character matches this description?
Laura, Mary, and Carrie's aunt, liked brown curls and golden curls.

Mix-N-Match

Character Cards
Little House in the Big Woods

Directions: Copy the Character Cards for *Little House in the Big Woods* by Laura Ingalls Wilder, one per student. Cut each card along the dotted line and follow the directions for Who Am I?.

① **Little House in the Big Woods**

Laura Ingalls

Who Am I?

② **Little House in the Big Woods**

Ma (Charlotte) Ingalls

Who Am I?

③ **Little House in the Big Woods**

Pa (Charles) Ingalls

Who Am I?

④ **Little House in the Big Woods**

Mary Ingalls

Who Am I?

Cooperative Learning & Literature
Kagan Publishing • (800) 933-2667 • www.KaganOnline.com

Character Cards
Little House in the Big Woods

Directions: Copy the Character Cards for *Little House in the Big Woods* by Laura Ingalls Wilder, one per student. Cut each card along the dotted line and follow the directions for Who Am I?.

⑤ Little House in the Big Woods

Charley

Who Am I?

⑥ Little House in the Big Woods

Grandpa Ingalls

Who Am I?

⑦ Little House in the Big Woods

Grandma Ingalls

Who Am I?

⑧ Little House in the Big Woods

Uncle Henry

Who Am I?

Character Cards
Little House in the Big Woods

Directions: Copy the Character Cards for *Little House in the Big Woods* by Laura Ingalls Wilder, one per student. Cut each card along the dotted line and follow the directions for Who Am I?.

⑨ Little House in the Big Woods

Aunt Polly

Who Am I?

⑩ Little House in the Big Woods

Baby Carrie

Who Am I?

⑪ Little House in the Big Woods

Jack

Who Am I?

⑫ Little House in the Big Woods

Aunt Lotty

Who Am I?

Cooperative Learning & Literature
Kagan Publishing • (800) 933-2667 • www.KaganOnline.com

Recall Questions
Little House in the Big Woods • Chapters 1–2

❏ **RallyCoach Directions:** Take turns answering each question as your partner coaches. Explain your thinking to your coach.

❏ **Sage-N-Scribe Directions:** The Sage describes what he or she knows about the question so the Scribe can answer the question. The Sage and Scribe switch roles for each question.

Little House in the Big Woods

Name _____

1. **Where does the story take place?**
   a. the prairie of Oklahoma
   b. the forest in Iowa
   c. the woods of Wisconsin
   d. a small town in Wyoming

2. **Why did Pa salt, smoke, and pack the venison away?**
   a. to take during his trip to town
   b. to trade in town for seeds
   c. to pay the landlord for the cabin
   d. to eat in the winter months

3. **What is most likely the author's reasoning for including specific details about gathering food?**
   a. to show where the Ingalls eat
   b. to demonstrate the hard work it takes to get food
   c. to persuade the reader to donate food
   d. to teach the reader about having a harvest

4. **Why was it necessary for Mary and Laura to play in the house?**
   a. The wolves were getting closer.
   b. The sun was no longer in the sky.
   c. The leaves were falling off the trees.
   d. The weather was getting colder.

5. **What chores does Laura like best in the Little House?**
   a. ironing and baking
   b. baking and churning
   c. reading and washing
   d. mending and churning

Little House in the Big Woods

Name _____

1. **What scared Laura about the woods at night?**
   a. The wolves would eat little girls.
   b. Ghosts were out looking for new families.
   c. It was too dark to see.
   d. Pa would not be able to find his way home.

2. **What did Pa mean when he said, "I saved the bacon?"**
   a. He prevented the pig from being eaten.
   b. He bought bacon at the town store.
   c. The bacon would be eaten in summer.
   d. The girls would save bacon for presents.

3. **What did Pa use the pig bladder for during Butchering Time?**
   a. as seasoning for the pig meat
   b. to measure the temperature of the oil
   c. as a ball to be kicked and bounced
   d. for gathering cracklings to fry

4. **How was Pa able to keep the bear meat fresh for a longer time?**
   a. He stored it in a refrigerator.
   b. It was so cold, the meat was frozen in the shed.
   c. Pa used salt and seasoning to keep it cool.
   d. The meat was hunted every day.

5. **What did Ma use for light late at night?**
   a. electric lamp
   b. moonlight
   c. kerosene lamp
   d. small flashlight

Recall Questions
Little House in the Big Woods • Chapters 3–4

❏ **RallyCoach Directions:** Take turns answering each question as your partner coaches. Explain your thinking to your coach.

❏ **Sage-N-Scribe Directions:** The Sage describes what he or she knows about the question so the Scribe can answer the question. The Sage and Scribe switch roles for each question.

Little House in the Big Woods

Name _____

1. What is most likely the author's reasoning for showing how Pa cares for his gun and bullets?
   a. to show how important the gun is to Pa
   b. to scare the reader from using guns
   c. to show how the gun was given to Pa
   d. to inform the reader about gun care

2. Why is it important to kill a wild animal on the first shot?
   a. It cost too much to use more bullets.
   b. It might scare the animal away.
   c. A gun weighed too much to hold for long.
   d. A wounded animal could kill a man before reloading his gun.

3. What was the cause of the "Who, Who" the young Pa heard in the woods?
   a. his brother playing a prank
   b. the barn door hitting the side of the barn
   c. his father calling him home
   d. a screech-owl in the trees

4. What Christmas present did Pa whittle for Ma?
   a. salt and pepper shakers
   b. a bracket for her China woman
   c. a long wooden spoon
   d. a tree ornament

5. What special present did Laura receive for Christmas?
   a. red scarf
   b. new petticoat
   c. knitted stockings
   d. rag doll

Little House in the Big Woods

Name _____

1. Where was the gun kept while Pa was at home?
   a. under the bed
   b. leaning next to the stove
   c. on hooks above the door
   d. in a special cabinet

2. During Pa's story, what prevented the young Pa from returning home once it got dark?
   a. He could not find his way.
   b. He dare not return without the cows.
   c. He was afraid of the dark.
   d. He knew he would be in trouble for missing dinner.

3. What lesson can Mary and Laura learn after listening to Pa tell his story?
   a. Always be home before dark.
   b. Obey your parents.
   c. Don't come home without the cows.
   d. Don't be afraid of the dark.

4. What was the true reason Prince growled at Aunt Eliza?
   a. Prince was bitten by a raccoon.
   b. Aunt Eliza was carrying bad furs.
   c. A panther was roaming near in the woods.
   d. Prince was scared of Aunt Eliza.

5. How did the cousins keep their fingers warm on the sleigh ride home?
   a. rough woolen mittens
   b. hot baked potatoes
   c. heated molasses
   d. extra layers of mittens

Recall Questions
Little House in the Big Woods • Chapters 5–6

❏ **RallyCoach Directions:** Take turns answering each question as your partner coaches. Explain your thinking to your coach.

❏ **Sage-N-Scribe Directions:** The Sage describes what he or she knows about the question so the Scribe can answer the question. The Sage and Scribe switch roles for each question.

Little House in the Big Woods

Name _____

1. **Why did Laura consider Sundays to be long?**
   a. She had to go to church all day.
   b. She was not allowed to speak.
   c. She must sit quietly and listen to stories.
   d. She had to do her schoolwork.

2. **In Pa's story what prevented the boys from finishing their sled before Sunday?**
   a. Their father kept them busy working, and they had chores.
   b. The boys did not have enough wood.
   c. Their father misplaced the wood tools.
   d. It began to rain and was too muddy.

3. **What lesson did Pa want the girls to learn from his story?**
   a. Stay away from wild hogs.
   b. It is easier to be good now than when Grandpa was a boy.
   c. Do not go sledding on a Sunday.
   d. Sundays are for reading and listening.

4. **What was Laura's job while helping her mom with the late-night milking?**
   a. opening and closing the gate
   b. holding the bucket for the milk
   c. watching baby Carrie
   d. carrying the lantern

5. **What presents did Pa bring back for Ma and the girls?**
   a. fresh bread
   b. pretty calico fabric
   c. new wooden spoons
   d. tin tea kettle

Little House in the Big Woods

Name _____

1. **What was the effect of Laura shouting, "I hate Sunday!"**
   a. She was sent to bed early.
   b. She recited an extra bedtime prayer.
   c. Pa told her a story about Grandpa's sled.
   d. She was allowed to play with dolls.

2. **What unexpected event happened when the boys went sledding?**
   a. They got lost in the woods.
   b. It snowed an extra foot at night.
   c. They ran into and picked up a hog.
   d. Pa caught the boys sledding down the hill.

3. **What was the reason Laura received a spanking on Monday morning?**
   a. It was her birthday.
   b. She did not help with morning chores.
   c. She yelled at Mary to get up.
   d. It was the first day of school.

4. **What did Ma and Laura encounter while going to milk Sukey?**
   a. a black bear
   b. a rabid raccoon
   c. a wilderness man
   d. wild horses

5. **What was the effect of Pa being late leaving from town?**
   a. He did not make it home until morning.
   b. He got lost in the woods and Ma found him.
   c. It was hard to see, and he thought a tree stump was a bear.
   d. He fell in the snow and got all wet.

Recall Questions
Little House in the Big Woods • Chapters 7–8

❑ **RallyCoach Directions:** Take turns answering each question as your partner coaches. Explain your thinking to your coach.

❑ **Sage-N-Scribe Directions:** The Sage describes what he or she knows about the question so the Scribe can answer the question. The Sage and Scribe switch roles for each question.

Little House in the Big Woods

Name _____

1. **Why does the author most likely include pictures in the book?**
   a. to teach the reader about the Big Woods
   b. to help the reader understand the old objects
   c. to persuade the reader to visit Laura
   d. to inform the reader about how to build a cabin

2. **What is sugar snow?**
   a. sugar and snow ice cream
   b. fine powder snow that looks like sugar
   c. the first snow of the winter
   d. a snow that means men can make more sugar

3. **What does the phrase "the beds were made by lamplight" mean in Chapter 8?**
   a. The family got up to leave before the sun.
   b. A dark storm is brewing outside.
   c. The lights were not working.
   d. A tree shaded the light in the windows.

4. **What conclusion can you make about the store soap the ladies used before the dance?**
   a. It was very common to find at the store.
   b. Everyone had a lot of it to use.
   c. It was a special soap to use for special times.
   d. It smelled lovely and made the skin white.

5. **Who was the best jigger at the dance?**
   a. Grandma
   b. Aunt Ruby
   c. Uncle George
   d. Grandpa

Little House in the Big Woods

Name _____

1. **How did Pa describe the tree sap?**
   a. the blood of the tree
   b. the treasure of the forest
   c. the life of the farm
   d. the secret of the prairie

2. **What excited Ma about going to Grandpa's cabin?**
   a. She liked to help bake bread for the winter.
   b. She got to wear her delaine dress.
   c. Laura would be able to play with her cousins.
   d. Pa would have help gathering grain.

3. **Why does Pa believe Uncle George is a wild man?**
   a. He lives alone in the woods.
   b. He is unmarried.
   c. He was once in war.
   d. He does not listen to the laws.

4. **What statement best describes how Laura felt during the dance at Grandpa's?**
   a. angry that she had to watch the little babies
   b. bored and lonely
   c. full of energy and hard to control
   d. in awe of the beautiful dresses and fun dances

5. **What did the children use the patty-pans for while at Grandma's?**
   a. to create music for the dance
   b. to bring in sugar from outside
   c. to eat Grandma's new syrup
   d. to play a game with the little children

Cooperative Learning & Literature
Kagan Publishing • (800) 933-2667 • www.KaganOnline.com

Recall Questions
Little House in the Big Woods • Chapters 9–10

❏ **RallyCoach Directions:** Take turns answering each question as your partner coaches. Explain your thinking to your coach.

❏ **Sage-N-Scribe Directions:** The Sage describes what he or she knows about the question so the Scribe can answer the question. The Sage and Scribe switch roles for each question.

Little House in the Big Woods

Name _____

1. **What conclusion can you make about why Laura could run only a little distance in bare feet?**
   a. There are sharp rocks by the little house.
   b. Ma did not like bare feet inside.
   c. Laura's feet were soft from wearing shoes.
   d. Laura might ruin her new oiled shoes.

2. **How far away is the nearest town?**
   a. 30 miles
   b. a 2-day walk
   c. 7 miles
   d. 17 miles

3. **How were the houses in town different from Laura's log cabin?**
   a. The town houses were larger with plumbing.
   b. The town houses were painted bright colors.
   c. The town houses were made of boards.
   d. The town houses had glass windows.

4. **What caused Laura's pocket to rip in the wagon?**
   a. a loose nail
   b. the weight of the rocks she collected
   c. a sharp twig along the shoreline
   d. Baby Carrie pulling on Laura

5. **Which of the following is NOT a summer chore for the ladies at the Little House?**
   a. gathering eggs
   b. weeding the garden
   c. picking berries
   d. making cheese

Little House in the Big Woods

Name _____

1. **What is the meaning of the word fawn found in Chapter 9?**
   a. momma deer
   b. baby deer
   c. wild deer
   d. color of a grown deer

2. **How did Laura feel when she saw the blue lake and sky overhead?**
   a. small and frightened
   b. small and wonderful
   c. full of energy and excitement
   d. frightened and alone

3. **What did Pa and Ma get for their trades at the store?**
   a. a new saddle for a horse
   b. a set of wooden spoons for Ma
   c. dark brown sugar for everyday use
   d. calico fabric for a new apron

4. **Why did Laura prefer to play with Clarence rather than Eva?**
   a. Eva was too bossy.
   b. Clarence was very short and babyish.
   c. Laura liked to run and climb trees too.
   d. Clarence was younger than Laura.

5. **What prevented the bees from stinging the black bear?**
   a. The bear was too large.
   b. The bees could not see the black bear.
   c. The bees could not get into the thick fur.
   d. The bear growled loudly.

Recall Questions
Little House in the Big Woods • Chapters 11–13

❑ **RallyCoach Directions:** Take turns answering each question as your partner coaches. Explain your thinking to your coach.

❑ **Sage-N-Scribe Directions:** The Sage describes what he or she knows about the question so the Scribe can answer the question. The Sage and Scribe switch roles for each question.

Little House in the Big Woods

Name _____

1. **What would happen if the oats were not in the stock before the rain came?**
   a. The oats would need to dry before trading.
   b. The crops would all be lost.
   c. The men would have to work in the rain.
   d. The rain would flood the fields making it hard to work.

2. **Which of the following was NOT something Charley did in the fields?**
   a. got in the men's way
   b. hid the whetstone
   c. brought the men fresh water
   d. screamed, pretending trouble

3. **What was Aunt Polly's remedy for Charley's yellow jacket stings?**
   a. extra cookies and fresh milk
   b. milkweed plaster casts and a warm bath
   c. salt scrub and essential oils
   d. mud plaster and a rolled-up sheet

4. **How long does it take to make hulled corn?**
   a. 3 weeks
   b. 2 or 3 days
   c. several hours
   d. 2 weeks

5. **How do the farmers pay the threshers who come to the farm?**
   a. with a referral to another farm
   b. stocks of grain
   c. sacks of wheat
   d. a night's rest and a warm breakfast

Little House in the Big Woods

Name _____

1. **Why did Pa believe Uncle Henry and Aunt Polly spoiled Charley?**
   a. Charley was not already working in the fields.
   b. Charley got everything he wanted at the store.
   c. Uncle Henry did not think Charley was strong.
   d. Aunt Polly cooked Charley his favorite foods.

2. **Why did the men not go to help Charley when he was screaming?**
   a. Charley was not very loud.
   b. The men were too far away.
   c. Charley had played tricks on the men earlier.
   d. The men did not like Charley.

3. **What does the author mean by the sentences, *"All the leaves stopped being green. They were yellow and scarlet and crimson."*?**
   a. It is very cold outside.
   b. It is beginning to become fall.
   c. Not enough water is available for the Big Woods.
   d. Pa took photos of the changing leaves.

4. **Why is the threshing machine referred to as an "eight-horsepower machine"?**
   a. It took eight horses to work the machine.
   b. The engine is known for being as strong as a horse.
   c. The machine is as large as eight horses.
   d. It takes eight horses to move the machine to another town.

5. **What was the reason Pa did not have fresh meat?**
   a. He could not find animals while hunting.
   b. He did not go to town to trade.
   c. He was busy loving the beauty of the animals.
   d. He worked hard in the fields and it got dark.

Cooperative Learning & Literature
Kagan Publishing • (800) 933-2667 • www.KaganOnline.com

Recall Questions
Little House in the Big Woods • End-of-Book

Directions: Copy one set of cards for each team. Cut out each card along the dotted line. Give each team a set of cards to play Fan-N-Pick or Showdown.

① Little House in the Big Woods

Why did Laura and Mary enjoy Butchering Time?

Fan-N-Pick/Showdown

② Little House in the Big Woods

What actually frightened Grandpa when he was alone in the Big Woods as a young boy?

Fan-N-Pick/Showdown

③ Little House in the Big Woods

What protected Aunt Eliza from the unknown panther by the spring?

Fan-N-Pick/Showdown

④ Little House in the Big Woods

How did Grandpa and his brothers disobey their father one Sunday?

Fan-N-Pick/Showdown

⑤ Little House in the Big Woods

Why did Ma want to trade for store sugar?

Fan-N-Pick/Showdown

⑥ Little House in the Big Woods

Where did Ma wear her special delaine dress?

Fan-N-Pick/Showdown

⑦ Little House in the Big Woods

What was actually the bear that Pa saw after trading his furs in town?

Fan-N-Pick/Showdown

⑧ Little House in the Big Woods

What caused Laura and Mary to take a bath in the middle of the week?

Fan-N-Pick/Showdown

Recall Questions
Little House in the Big Woods • End-of-Book

Directions: Copy one set of cards for each team. Cut out each card along the dotted line. Give each team a set of cards to play Fan-N-Pick or Showdown.

⑨ Little House in the Big Woods Why did Laura cry before leaving town?	**⑩ Little House in the Big Woods** What was the reason Uncle Henry and Pa did not help Charley in the fields?
⑪ Little House in the Big Woods What caused Laura to slap Mary?	**⑫ Little House in the Big Woods** What surprise did Ma and Laura discover when going to milk Sukey late one night?
⑬ Little House in the Big Woods Grandma made something called hasty pudding. What is hasty pudding?	**⑭ Little House in the Big Woods** What did the men call the sap found in the trees?
⑮ Little House in the Big Woods Why were Mary and Laura so excited to go to town with Pa?	**⑯ Little House in the Big Woods** What were the girls forbidden to do on Sundays?

Cooperative Learning & Literature
Kagan Publishing • (800) 933-2667 • www.KaganOnline.com

Journal Writing
Little House in the Big Woods • Chapter 1

Directions: Think about the Journal Question, and then write your own response. When done, RoundRobin share your writing with your teammates. Use the space at the bottom to record ideas your teammates share.

Journal Question
What conclusions can you make about life at the Ingalls' home in the Big Woods? Use story details to justify your answer.

Journal Response: _____

_____

_____

_____

_____

_____

_____

_____

_____

_____

_____

_____

Ideas Teammates Shared

Journal Writing
Little House in the Big Woods • Chapter 3

Directions: Think about the Journal Question, and then write your own response. When done, RoundRobin share your writing with your teammates. Use the space at the bottom to record ideas your teammates share.

Journal Question
Describe the importance of each family member's responsibility in the Ingalls' home. Could they survive without each other? Explain and justify.

Journal Response: _____

_____

_____

_____

_____

_____

_____

_____

_____

_____

_____

_____

Ideas Teammates Shared

Cooperative Learning & Literature
Kagan Publishing • (800) 933-2667 • www.KaganOnline.com

Journal Writing
Little House in the Big Woods • Chapter 8

Directions: Think about the Journal Question, and then write your own response. When done, RoundRobin share your writing with your teammates. Use the space at the bottom to record ideas your teammates share.

Journal Question
The ladies and gentlemen take great care in preparing for the dance at Grandpa and Grandma's house. They use special soap and wear fancy dresses. In your opinion, why do you think this time together is so special? Explain and justify.

Journal Response: _____

_____

_____

_____

_____

_____

_____

_____

_____

_____

_____

_____

_____

Ideas Teammates Shared

Journal Writing
Little House in the Big Woods • Chapter 12

Directions: Think about the Journal Question, and then write your own response. When done, RoundRobin share your writing with your teammates. Use the space at the bottom to record ideas your teammates share.

Journal Question
Pa said, "*It served the little liar right,*" when referring to Charley being stung by yellow jackets. Is this statement true? Support your thinking with details.

Journal Response: _____

_____

_____

_____

_____

_____

_____

_____

_____

_____

_____

_____

Ideas Teammates Shared

Journal Writing
Little House in the Big Woods • End-of-Book

Directions: Think about the Journal Question, and then write your own response. When done, RoundRobin share your writing with your teammates. Use the space at the bottom to record ideas your teammates share.

Journal Question
If you could send one item back in time to Ma, Pa, Laura, Baby Carrie, and Mary, what would you send each member of the Ingalls' Family?

Journal Response: _____

_____

_____

_____

_____

_____

_____

_____

_____

_____

_____

_____

Ideas Teammates Shared

Higher-Level Thinking Cards
Little House in the Big Woods

Directions: Copy enough cards so that each student receives a Question Card. Have students stand up, pair up, and do Traveling Pair Share to respond to each other's questions. Students trade cards and find a new partner to share.

① **Little House in the Big Woods**

Why does the author spend a lot of time describing with great detail the daily life in the Ingalls' home?

Traveling Pair Share

② **Little House in the Big Woods**

How do the stories Pa tells the girls help the reader understand the story?

Traveling Pair Share

③ **Little House in the Big Woods**

Think about how life in the Big Woods was for the Ingalls family. Do they need each other to survive? Explain.

Traveling Pair Share

④ **Little House in the Big Woods**

Pa is very strict with Laura and Mary. How do his expectations protect the girls? How do these expectations differ from your life?

Traveling Pair Share

⑤ **Little House in the Big Woods**

After reading about how hard life is in the Big Woods, what do you take away as easy today?

Traveling Pair Share

⑥ **Little House in the Big Woods**

What inventions would Pa enjoy that we have today? Justify and explain.

Traveling Pair Share

⑦ **Little House in the Big Woods**

If you could go back in time and spend a week with the Ingalls family, what three items would you like to have and why?

Traveling Pair Share

⑧ **Little House in the Big Woods**

What lessons does Pa teach the girls? Why are these important to survival?

Traveling Pair Share

Cooperative Learning & Literature
Kagan Publishing • (800) 933-2667 • www.KaganOnline.com

Higher-Level Thinking Cards
Little House in the Big Woods

Directions: Copy enough cards so that each student receives a Question Card. Have students stand up, pair up, and do Traveling Pair Share to respond to each other's questions. Students trade cards and find a new partner to share.

9 Little House in the Big Woods

Who is the hardest worker in the Ingalls family? Explain.

Traveling Pair Share

10 Little House in the Big Woods

The girls do not go to school. Is school important for Laura and Mary? Explain.

Traveling Pair Share

11 Little House in the Big Woods

How do the characters in the story show cooperation? Why is cooperation important to those living in the Big Woods?

Traveling Pair Share

12 Little House in the Big Woods

Pa plays the fiddle to the girls at night. How do you think he learned to play this instrument? Explain your thinking.

Traveling Pair Share

13 Little House in the Big Woods

How could the weather affect the lives of those in the Big Woods? Explain.

Traveling Pair Share

14 Little House in the Big Woods

Pa is thrilled with the help of the threshing machine. If Pa were alive today, with what machine would he be the most impressed?

Traveling Pair Share

15 Little House in the Big Woods

Describe Ma's role in the survival of the Ingalls family. Why is she so important?

Traveling Pair Share

16 Little House in the Big Woods

Are Pa and Ma good role models for Laura and Mary? Explain your thinking.

Traveling Pair Share

Higher-Level Thinking Cards
Little House in the Big Woods

Directions: Copy enough cards so that each student receives a Question Card. Have students stand up, pair up, and do Traveling Pair Share to respond to each other's questions. Students trade cards and find a new partner to share.

17 Little House in the Big Woods

If you could ask Laura any question, what would it be and why?

Traveling Pair Share

18 Little House in the Big Woods

Items such as new fabric, store sugar, and store soap are very precious to the Ingalls. These items are *very simple*. Why are they so important?

Traveling Pair Share

19 Little House in the Big Woods

How does your family compare to the Ingalls family? Explain.

Traveling Pair Share

20 Little House in the Big Woods

In your opinion, is Pa too strict with Laura and Mary? Explain.

Traveling Pair Share

21 Little House in the Big Woods

Would you like to spend a month living with the Ingalls family? Why or why not?

Traveling Pair Share

22 Little House in the Big Woods

What is something new you learned after reading *Little House in the Big Woods*?

Traveling Pair Share

23 Little House in the Big Woods

Laura was excited to see a town for the first time. How do you think Laura would react to seeing a large city? Scared? Excited? Explain your thinking.

Traveling Pair Share

24 Little House in the Big Woods

If Laura could come visit you, what game or toy would you show her? Why? Explain your thinking.

Traveling Pair Share

Cooperative Learning & Literature
Kagan Publishing • (800) 933-2667 • www.KaganOnline.com

Ramona Quimby, Age 8

By Beverly Cleary

Ramona is a young 3rd grader starting a new school year in a new school. She gets embarrassed when she cracks an egg on her head and finds out it is raw. Ramona thinks her teacher Mrs. Whaley called her a show-off and a nuisance. Her favorite part of the day, however, is sustained reading, which helps her to like school. Ramona can see that her family is struggling financially and is concerned. She knows they are still a happy family and she uses her creative ways to help them out. This is a heartwarming story with silliness and lessons learned.

Reading Level

Lexile Level: 740L
Guided Reading Level: O
DRA Level: 38
Accelerated Reader: 4.6

Ramona Quimby, Age 8

~ Cooperative Learning Activities ~

Character and Description Cards
Ramona Quimby, Age 8

Directions: Cut out each card along the dotted line. Matching cards are presented side by side in the book. Give each student one matching card to play Mix-N-Match.

Ramona Quimby, Age 8
How would you describe this character?
Ramona Quimby

Mix-N-Match

Ramona Quimby, Age 8
Which character matches this description?
The main character of the story who is 8 years old and the youngest member of the Quimby family, worries about her family and about being a show-off.

Mix-N-Match

Ramona Quimby, Age 8
How would you describe this character?
Beezus Quimby

Mix-N-Match

Ramona Quimby, Age 8
Which character matches this description?
The oldest daughter in the Quimby family who has just started junior high school, has a lot of homework to do and likes to go to sleepovers.

Mix-N-Match

Ramona Quimby, Age 8
How would you describe this character?
Danny (Yard Ape)

Mix-N-Match

Ramona Quimby, Age 8
Which character matches this description?
Meets Ramona on the bus the first day and takes her eraser, continues to bully Ramona at school but is starting to be a friend.

Mix-N-Match

Ramona Quimby, Age 8
How would you describe this character?
Mrs. Quimby

Mix-N-Match

Ramona Quimby, Age 8
Which character matches this description?
The mother of the family and works as a secretary at a doctor's office, stays home with Ramona when she is sick.

Mix-N-Match

Character and Description Cards
Ramona Quimby, Age 8

Directions: Cut out each card along the dotted line. Matching cards are presented side by side in the book. Give each student one matching card to play Mix-N-Match.

Ramona Quimby, Age 8
How would you describe this character?
Mr. Quimby

Ramona Quimby, Age 8
Which character matches this description?
Worked at a supermarket and in the freezer as "Santa's Little Helper" according to Ramona, went back to college to be an art teacher.

Ramona Quimby, Age 8
How would you describe this character?
Howie Kemp

Ramona Quimby, Age 8
Which character matches this description?
Grandson of Mrs. Kemp, owns a bike and likes to ride it, rides the school bus with Ramona.

Ramona Quimby, Age 8
How would you describe this character?
Willa Jean Kemp

Ramona Quimby, Age 8
Which character matches this description?
6-year old granddaughter of Mrs. Kemp, Ramona struggles to get along with her, wants to play, excited to be starting kindergarten.

Ramona Quimby, Age 8
How would you describe this character?
Mrs. Whaley

Ramona Quimby, Age 8
Which character matches this description?
Ramona's 3rd grade teacher, states her name is like the animal but with a "y," calls Ramona a nuisance and a show-off.

Cooperative Learning & Literature
Kagan Publishing • (800) 933-2667 • www.KaganOnline.com

Character and Description Cards
Ramona Quimby, Age 8

Directions: Cut out each card along the dotted line. Matching cards are presented side by side in the book. Give each student one matching card to play Mix-N-Match.

Ramona Quimby, Age 8

How would you describe this character?
Mrs. Kemp

Mix-N-Match

Ramona Quimby, Age 8

Which character matches this description?
Watches Ramona after school, grandmother to Howie and Willa Jean, says Ramona does not try hard enough to be nice.

Mix-N-Match

Ramona Quimby, Age 8

How would you describe this character?
Mrs. Larson

Mix-N-Match

Ramona Quimby, Age 8

Which character matches this description?
The school secretary who had to get the egg out of Ramona's hair, helped Ramona feel better after she got sick.

Mix-N-Match

Ramona Quimby, Age 8

How would you describe this character?
Old Man

Mix-N-Match

Ramona Quimby, Age 8

Which character matches this description?
A mysterious person who paid for the Quimby's dinner, asked Ramona if she has been good to her mother.

Mix-N-Match

Ramona Quimby, Age 8

How would you describe this character?
Beverly Cleary

Mix-N-Match

Ramona Quimby, Age 8

Which character matches this description?
Author of the *Ramona Quimby* series, winner of the John Newberry Medal.

Mix-N-Match

Character Cards
Ramona Quimby, Age 8

Directions: Copy the Character Cards for *Ramona Quimby, Age 8* by Beverly Cleary, one per student. Cut each card along the dotted line and follow the directions for Who Am I?.

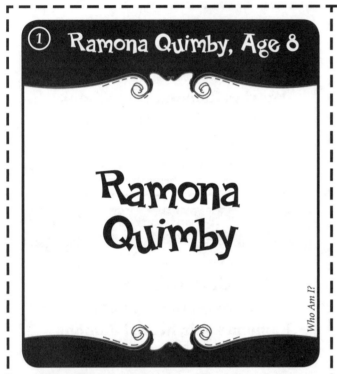

① **Ramona Quimby, Age 8**

Ramona Quimby

Who Am I?

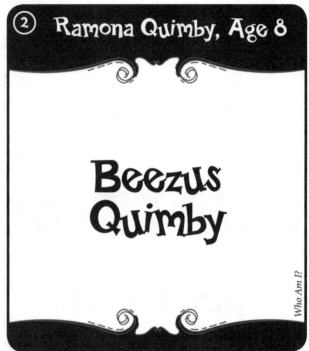

② **Ramona Quimby, Age 8**

Beezus Quimby

Who Am I?

③ **Ramona Quimby, Age 8**

Danny (Yard Ape)

Who Am I?

④ **Ramona Quimby, Age 8**

Mrs. Quimby

Who Am I?

Character Cards
Ramona Quimby, Age 8

Directions: Copy the Character Cards for *Ramona Quimby, Age 8* by Beverly Cleary, one per student. Cut each card along the dotted line and follow the directions for Who Am I?.

⑤ Ramona Quimby, Age 8

Mr. Quimby

Who Am I?

⑥ Ramona Quimby, Age 8

Howie Kemp

Who Am I?

⑦ Ramona Quimby, Age 8

Willa Jean Kemp

Who Am I?

⑧ Ramona Quimby, Age 8

Mrs. Whaley

Who Am I?

Character Cards
Ramona Quimby, Age 8

Directions: Copy the Character Cards for *Ramona Quimby, Age 8* by Beverly Cleary, one per student. Cut each card along the dotted line and follow the directions for Who Am I?.

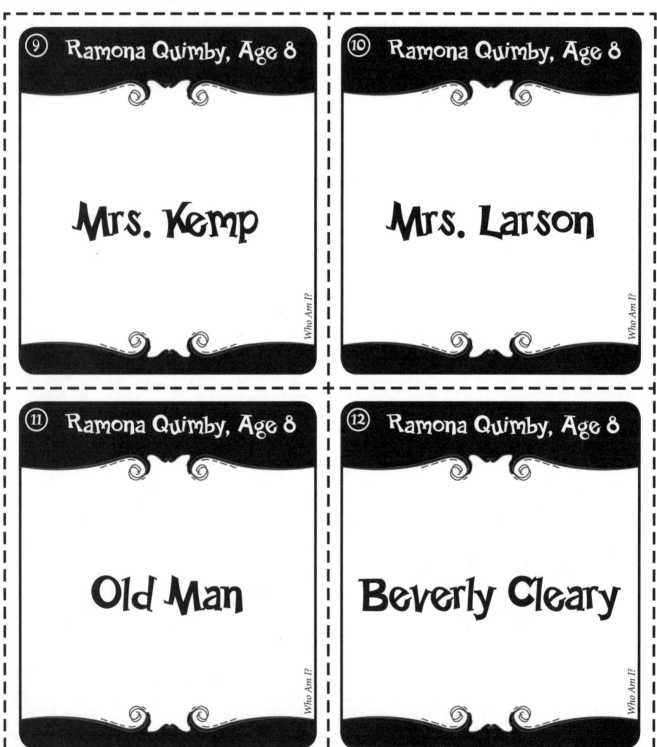

⑨ Ramona Quimby, Age 8

Mrs. Kemp

Who Am I?

⑩ Ramona Quimby, Age 8

Mrs. Larson

Who Am I?

⑪ Ramona Quimby, Age 8

Old Man

Who Am I?

⑫ Ramona Quimby, Age 8

Beverly Cleary

Who Am I?

Cooperative Learning & Literature
Kagan Publishing • (800) 933-2667 • www.KaganOnline.com

Recall Questions
Ramona Quimby, Age 8 • Chapters 1–2

❑ **RallyCoach Directions:** Take turns answering each question as your partner coaches. Explain your thinking to your coach.

❑ **Sage-N-Scribe Directions:** The Sage describes what he or she knows about the question so the Scribe can answer the question. The Sage and Scribe switch roles for each question.

Name _____

1. What worry did Ramona have about riding the bus to school?
   a. getting carsick
   b. sitting next to Danny
   c. being left at school
   d. not having a seat

2. What did Ramona's father give her before going to school?
   a. a new pencil
   b. a purple pen
   c. a pearly pink eraser
   d. a plastic backpack

3. Who bullied Ramona on the school bus?
   a. Mrs. Hanna
   b. Howie
   c. Willa Jean
   d. Danny

4. What conclusion can you make about how Ramona feels about school?
   a. Ramona likes to solve math problems.
   b. Ramona does not like the class pet.
   c. Ramona's favorite time of day is reading.
   d. Ramona sings in the school choir.

5. What animal did Willa Jean ask Ramona to be during the dress-up game?
   a. dog
   b. rat
   c. mouse
   d. cat

Name _____

1. Where did Mr. Quimby work before returning to school?
   a. the local fast-food restaurant
   b. the food court at the mall
   c. the check-out counter at Shop-Rite Market
   d. the gift shop at the hospital

2. Where does Ramona go after school?
   a. straight home
   b. Mrs. Kemp's house
   c. church daycare
   d. to her mother's work

3. What nickname did Ramona accidently give herself?
   a. Little Bigfoot
   b. Superfoot
   c. Yard Ape
   d. Squeaky Toes

4. What does DEAR stand for?
   a. Don't Eat a Reader
   b. Do Everything Always Right
   c. Drop Everything and Run
   d. Drop Everything and Read

5. How was Ramona finally able to avoid playing with Willa Jean?
   a. Willa Jean had to take a nap.
   b. Bruce wanted to play in the sandbox.
   c. Ramona said she needed to do her Sustained Silent Reading.
   d. Beezus asked Ramona to come back home.

Recall Questions
Ramona Quimby, Age 8 • Chapters 3–4

❏ **RallyCoach Directions:** Take turns answering each question as your partner coaches. Explain your thinking to your coach.

❏ **Sage-N-Scribe Directions:** The Sage describes what he or she knows about the question so the Scribe can answer the question. The Sage and Scribe switch roles for each question.

Name _____

1. What food item does Ramona ask her mother to put in her lunch box?
a. a raw egg
b. a shiny new apple
c. a bag of chips
d. a hard-boiled egg

2. What was the reason for the oatmeal to be dyed blue?
a. to warn students not to eat the oatmeal
b. to match the school color blue
c. so the students could see the larvae
d. to monitor the change of blue oatmeal

3. What did Ramona hear while in the nurse's office?
a. Mrs. Whaley calling Ramona a show-off.
b. Mrs. Whaley asking if she could go home.
c. The teachers talking about the rainy weather.
d. The secretary telling Mrs. Whaley how sweet Ramona is today.

4. What meat did Mrs. Quimby serve for dinner?
a. pot roast
b. hamburger
c. tongue
d. frog legs

5. Why did Beezus not want to look at the food in the refrigerator?
a. She did not want to be in trouble for getting out of bed.
b. She did not want her parents to think they were hungry.
c. She wanted to read.
d. Ramona was not allowed downstairs.

Name _____

1. What is the meaning of the word fad found in the story?
a. a popular thing to do
b. a type of egg
c. a place to go eat your lunch
d. a word to describe math homework

2. What conclusion can you make after Ramona's lunch period?
a. She is excited to have a hard-boiled egg.
b. The teachers will ban eggs from lunch.
c. She is embarrassed about the egg in her hair.
d. The principal will give Ramona detention.

3. What art assignment was Ramona's father working on when she got home?
a. drawing a picture of the cat
b. coloring design of multiple colors
c. drawing a picture of his foot
d. taking a snapshot of the family

4. What was the result of Ramona and Beezus's reaction to the food?
a. They have to cook dinner on the weekend.
b. They did not get any dessert.
c. They were grounded for 1 week.
d. They were sent straight to bed.

5. What did the girls decide to do in order to help their parents forget about their punishment?
a. talk to their grandmother
b. complain about having lots of homework
c. offer to do dishes the whole week
d. try to be extra good

Cooperative Learning & Literature
Kagan Publishing • (800) 933-2667 • www.KaganOnline.com

Recall Questions
Ramona Quimby, Age 8 • Chapters 5–6

❏ **RallyCoach Directions:** Take turns answering each question as your partner coaches. Explain your thinking to your coach.

❏ **Sage-N-Scribe Directions:** The Sage describes what he or she knows about the question so the Scribe can answer the question. The Sage and Scribe switch roles for each question.

Name _____

1. Which of the following is NOT something the girls did to be extra good on Sunday?
a. clean their room
b. compliment their mother's French toast
c. go to Sunday school neat and combed
d. bring the newspaper in to their dad

2. What did the girls use in their recipe to make the little specks?
a. pakrika
b. red pepper flakes
c. chili powder
d. cinnamon

3. What conclusion can you make about the mess in the kitchen?
a. Mrs. Quimby had trouble making dinner.
b. The girls will not be allowed to cook again.
c. It will take a while to get the kitchen clean.
d. Mr. Quimby will go to work.

4. What terrible, horrible, dreadful, awful thing happened to Ramona at school?
a. Mrs. Whaley asked her to answer a problem.
b. Ramona threw up on the floor.
c. Ramona forgot to do her homework.
d. Yard Ape called Ramona Deviled Egghead.

5. How did Ramona get back home?
a. Howie's grandmother's pick-up truck
b. the city bus
c. a taxi
d. Mrs. Quimby's boss's car

Name _____

1. Why is Chapter 5 most likely titled *The Extra-Good Sunday*?
a. The girls resolved to be extra good on Sunday.
b. The parents took the girls to a special movie.
c. The girls did not have to do their chores.
d. The grandparents came into town.

2. What did Ramona spill on the floor that made the *grit, grit, grit* sound?
a. peach syrup
b. candle wax
c. cream of wheat
d. chicken skin

3. Why was Mrs. Quimby needed to steer the car?
a. Mr. Quimby couldn't see out the back window.
b. The girls had smeared mud on the tires.
c. Mrs. Quimby was a better driver.
d. The car could not go into reverse.

4. Who came to pick up Ramona from the office?
a. Mrs. Quimby
b. Mrs. Larson
c. Beezus
d. Howie Kemp's grandmother

5. What conclusion can you make about the fizzy drink Mrs. Quimby gave Ramona?
a. It is probably a soda.
b. It is only water.
c. It will make her throw up some more.
d. It has special medicine in it.

Recall Questions
Ramona Quimby, Age 8 • Chapters 7–9

❏ **RallyCoach Directions:** Take turns answering each question as your partner coaches. Explain your thinking to your coach.

❏ **Sage-N-Scribe Directions:** The Sage describes what he or she knows about the question so the Scribe can answer the question. The Sage and Scribe switch roles for each question.

Name _____

1. What did Ramona find on her bedside table when she woke up in the morning?
a. milk and toast
b. a cartoon drawn by her father
c. the Sunday newspaper
d. her DEAR book

2. According to Mrs. Quimby, what normally causes Picky-Picky to avoid Ramona?
a. Ramona is noisy.
b. Ramona's room is always messy.
c. Ramona is sick and might throw up.
d. Ramona does not like cats.

3. What suggestion did Mr. Quimby make to Ramona regarding her book report?
a. Pretend it is a new movie.
b. Make it into a commercial.
c. Put on a play of the best scene.
d. Do not tell the ending to the class.

4. What was the cause of the Quimby family being in a bad mood on Sunday?
a. The weather was dreary and rainy.
b. Mr. Quimby lost his job as Santa's Little Helper.
c. Beezus was now sick with the stomach flu.
d. Ramona and Mrs. Quimby were not talking.

5. What was Mr. Quimby's solution to the Quimby's dreary Sunday?
a. going for a walk in the park
b. going out to dinner
c. driving around looking at gardens
d. seeing a movie at the drive-in

Name _____

1. Which two words best describe Ramona during her sick day?
a. tired and happy
b. playful and angry
c. sick and energetic
d. bored and cranky

2. What did Ramona's friend, Sara, bring her after school?
a. Ramona's pink eraser
b. some letters and a book
c. the jar of fruit flies and blue oatmeal
d. math homework and a science book

3. What was the result of Ramona, Janet, and Sara wearing the cat masks during the report?
a. Ramona failed her report.
b. Mrs. Whaley sent Ramona to the principal.
c. Ramona kept giggling and forgot her words.
d. The class was told not to read the book.

4. What conclusion can you make about Ramona's room?
a. The room is very neat and tidy.
b. Ramona's room is right next to the bathroom.
c. Picky-Picky has his own corner for napping.
d. Ramona has a very messy room.

5. What was the old man's reason for paying for the Quimby's meal?
a. Ramona said she was good to her mom.
b. He heard Mr. Quimby complain about money.
c. The Quimby's looked like a nice family.
d. Beezus knew the old man's grandson.

Cooperative Learning & Literature
Kagan Publishing • (800) 933-2667 • www.KaganOnline.com

Recall Questions
Ramona Quimby, Age 8 • End-of-Book

Directions: Participate in Find Someone Who to answer the recall questions about *Ramona Quimby, Age 8*. Circle the correct answer provided by your partner and have your partner initial the answer.

1 Why did Mr. Quimby return to college?

a. He lost his job at the market.
b. He wants to be an art teacher.
c. He is teaching a history class.

Initials _____

2 What was the old man's reason for paying for the Quimby's meal?

a. Ramona thanked her mom.
b. The family looked nice.
c. Mr. Quimby could not pay.

Initials _____

3 Why did Ramona hit an egg on her head at lunch?

a. She was dared to.
b. She wanted to be sent home.
c. It was the latest fad for 3rd graders.

Initials _____

4 Where did Mr. Quimby take the family at the end of the book?

a. out for ice cream
b. to a drive-in movie
c. out for dinner
d. a walk in the park

Initials _____

5 What nickname did Ramona accidently give herself?

a. Yard Ape
b. Superfoot
c. Egghead
d. Squeaky

Initials _____

6 Who stayed with Ramona when she was sick?

a. Howie's grandmother
b. Beezus
c. Mrs. Quimby

Initials _____

7 What did Ramona hear while in the office?

a. Mrs. Whaley quit teaching.
b. Mrs. Whaley call Ramona a show-off and nuisance.
c. Mrs. Larson calling her parents.

Initials _____

8 What did Mr. Quimby give Ramona on her first day of school?

a. a tin lunch box
b. a shiny, pink eraser
c. new sandals

Initials _____

9 Why did Ramona and Beezus have to cook Sunday dinner?

a. Mrs. Quimby had to work late.
b. Mr. Quimby had a late class.
c. The girls complained about the tongue.

Initials _____

10 What does DEAR stand for?

a. Don't Eat a Reader
b. Drop Everything and Read
c. Drop Everything and Run

Initials _____

11 What terrible, horrible, awful thing happened at school requiring Mrs. Quimby to get Ramona?

a. She threw up on the floor.
b. She got into a fight with Yard Ape.
c. She refused to do her schoolwork.

Initials _____

12 Where did Ramona go after school?

a. the local daycare
b. home with Beezus
c. Mrs. Kemp's house

Initials _____

Journal Writing
Ramona Quimby, Age 8 • Chapter 2

Directions: Think about the Journal Question, and then write your own response. When done, RoundRobin share your writing with your teammates. Use the space at the bottom to record ideas your teammates share.

Journal Question
Do you think it is a good decision to send Ramona to Willa Jean's grandma's house after school? Explain your thinking.

Journal Response: _____

_____

_____

_____

_____

_____

_____

_____

_____

_____

_____

Ideas Teammates Shared

Cooperative Learning & Literature
Kagan Publishing • (800) 933-2667 • www.KaganOnline.com

Journal Writing
Ramona Quimby, Age 8 • Chapter 4

Directions: Think about the Journal Question, and then write your own response. When done, RoundRobin share your writing with your teammates. Use the space at the bottom to record ideas your teammates share.

Journal Question
Ramona chooses to participate in the new 3rd grade fad of bringing hard-boiled eggs even though she doesn't like hard-boiled eggs. Have you ever done something you did not like because it was popular? Explain.

Journal Response: _____

_____

_____

_____

_____

_____

_____

_____

_____

_____

_____

_____

Ideas Teammates Shared

Journal Writing
Ramona Quimby, Age 8 • Chapter 6

Directions: Think about the Journal Question, and then write your own response. When done, RoundRobin share your writing with your teammates. Use the space at the bottom to record ideas your teammates share.

Journal Question
Was it a good punishment to make the girls cook dinner after complaining about the tongue?
Why or why not? Explain your thinking.

Journal Response: _____

_____

_____

_____

_____

_____

_____

_____

_____

_____

_____

_____

_____

Ideas Teammates Shared

Cooperative Learning & Literature
Kagan Publishing • (800) 933-2667 • www.KaganOnline.com

Journal Writing
Ramona Quimby, Age 8 • Chapter 9

Directions: Think about the Journal Question, and then write your own response. When done, RoundRobin share your writing with your teammates. Use the space at the bottom to record ideas your teammates share.

Journal Question
What do you predict will happen after the story ends for Ramona and her family? Explain your thinking using story details.

Journal Response: _____

_____

_____

_____

_____

_____

_____

_____

_____

_____

_____

_____

Ideas Teammates Shared

Higher-Level Thinking Cards
Ramona Quimby, Age 8

Directions: Copy enough cards so that each student receives a Question Card. Have students stand up, pair up, and do Traveling Pair Share to respond to each other's questions. Students trade cards and find a new partner to share.

① **Ramona Quimby, Age 8**

It was a fad to bring a hard-boiled egg to school. What is a fad at your school? Explain.

Traveling Pair Share

② **Ramona Quimby, Age 8**

When does this story take place (past, present, or future)? How do you know? Explain.

Traveling Pair Share

③ **Ramona Quimby, Age 8**

What lesson can you learn after reading *Ramona Quimby, Age 8*? Justify.

Traveling Pair Share

④ **Ramona Quimby, Age 8**

Is it a good decision to send Ramona to Mrs. Kemp's house after school?

Traveling Pair Share

⑤ **Ramona Quimby, Age 8**

Was Mr. Quimby's solution to the family's dreary Sunday a good decision? Evaluate and explain.

Traveling Pair Share

⑥ **Ramona Quimby, Age 8**

Do you think it is a good idea for Mr. Quimby to return to college? Evaluate and explain.

Traveling Pair Share

⑦ **Ramona Quimby, Age 8**

Do you predict Ramona and Danny will become friends? Justify your answer.

Traveling Pair Share

⑧ **Ramona Quimby, Age 8**

Ramona likes to read during the class. What is your favorite thing to do in school?

Traveling Pair Share

Higher-Level Thinking Cards
Ramona Quimby, Age 8

Directions: Copy enough cards so that each student receives a Question Card. Have students stand up, pair up, and do Traveling Pair Share to respond to each other's questions. Students trade cards and find a new partner to share.

⑨ Ramona Quimby, Age 8

Which character are you the most alike in this book? Please explain.

Traveling Pair Share

⑩ Ramona Quimby, Age 8

Why did the pink eraser mean so much to Ramona? Explain.

Traveling Pair Share

⑪ Ramona Quimby, Age 8

What do you think will happen as a result of the mess in the kitchen?

Traveling Pair Share

⑫ Ramona Quimby, Age 8

Was it a good punishment to make the girls cook dinner? Justify and Explain.

Traveling Pair Share

⑬ Ramona Quimby, Age 8

Did Mr. and Mrs. Quimby's punishment over the tongue work? Why or why not?

Traveling Pair Share

⑭ Ramona Quimby, Age 8

How does Ramona change from the beginning of the book to the end of the book? Explain.

Traveling Pair Share

⑮ Ramona Quimby, Age 8

Ramona worries about her family. What are some ways Ramona can help her family?

Traveling Pair Share

⑯ Ramona Quimby, Age 8

Describe the relationship between Ramona and Beezus.

Traveling Pair Share

Higher-Level Thinking Cards
Ramona Quimby, Age 8

Directions: Copy enough cards so that each student receives a Question Card. Have students stand up, pair up, and do Traveling Pair Share to respond to each other's questions. Students trade cards and find a new partner to share.

⑰ Ramona Quimby, Age 8

What is the most important event in the story? Please explain why it is important.

Traveling Pair Share

⑱ Ramona Quimby, Age 8

In what ways are you and Ramona alike? Explain.

Traveling Pair Share

⑲ Ramona Quimby, Age 8

In what ways are you and Ramona different? Explain.

Traveling Pair Share

⑳ Ramona Quimby, Age 8

How would the story be different if Mr. Quimby did not return to school?

Traveling Pair Share

㉑ Ramona Quimby, Age 8

What reactions did you have to Mrs. Whaley calling Ramona a show-off and a nuisance?

Traveling Pair Share

㉒ Ramona Quimby, Age 8

How did Ramona solve her problem with Mrs. Whaley?

Traveling Pair Share

㉓ Ramona Quimby, Age 8

What advice would you give Ramona on how to deal with bullies at school?

Traveling Pair Share

㉔ Ramona Quimby, Age 8

Would you like to be friends with Ramona? Why or why not? Explain.

Traveling Pair Share

Cooperative Learning & Literature
Kagan Publishing • (800) 933-2667 • www.KaganOnline.com

The Ravenmaster's Secret: Escape from the Tower of London

By Elvira Woodruff

Forrest Harper and his ravens lived somewhere horrible, maybe even frightening. The time was 1735, and the place was the Tower of London. Forrest was bored doing the same chores day in and day out, until one day when Scottish Rebels were captured, his life changed. He was excited that he would now be able to show his bravery. It turns out Forrest is to guard the Rebel's young daughter, Maddy, who is also charged with treason and could be killed for her crimes. They become friends and he finds himself in a moral predicament, making decisions that may hurt him in the long run.

The Ravenmaster's Secret: Escape from the Tower of London

∽ Cooperative Learning Activities ∽

Cooperative Learning & Literature
Kagan Publishing • (800) 933-2667 • www.KaganOnline.com

Recall Questions

The Ravenmaster's Secret: Escape from the Tower of London • Chapers I–V

Directions: Participate in Find Someone Who to answer the recall questions about *The Ravenmaster's Secret: Escape from the Tower of London*. Circle the correct answer provided by your partner and have your partner initial the answer.

1 **What were the guards called who worked at the Tower of London?**

a. Yeoman Warders
b. Tower Guards
c. Chosen Warders
d. King's Guards

_____ Initials

2 **According to ancient legend, what would happen if the ravens were removed from the Tower?**

a. The Tower would be overrun with rats.
b. The Tower would fall to the enemies.
c. The Tower would become rich with wealth.
d. The Tower would be infected with the plague.

_____ Initials

3 **When does this story take place?**

a. 1834
b. 1625
c. 1735
d. 1922

_____ Initials

4 **What caused the powerful stench at the Tower?**

a. raw onions cooking
b. rats feeding on the dead animals
c. unclean Tower guards
d. chamber pots being emptied into the river

_____ Initials

5 **What is collar day?**

a. hanging day
b. washing day
c. feast day
d. school day

_____ Initials

6 **Why did Finch and Whipley call Forrest "Hare Hart"?**

a. He was fast like a rabbit.
b. He grew pale and fainted.
c. He threw up when he saw the hanging.
d. He was carrying his younger sister Bea.

_____ Initials

7 **What did the *clang, clang, clang* from the Bell Tower mean?**

a. A prisoner had escaped.
b. The guards were changing.
c. All gates would soon be locked.
d. The drawbridge is open.

_____ Initials

8 **According to Forrest's father, what is the source of a man's strength?**

a. a wise mind
b. his character
c. strong work ethic
d. perseverance

_____ Initials

9 **What genre is the story of *The Ravenmaster's Secret: Escape from the Tower of London*?**

a. nonfiction
b. science fiction
c. fantasy
d. historical fiction

_____ Initials

Recall Questions

The Ravenmaster's Secret: Escape from the Tower of London • Chapers VI–XI

Directions: Participate in Find Someone Who to answer the recall questions about *The Ravenmaster's Secret: Escape from the Tower of London*. Circle the correct answer provided by your partner and have your partner initial the answer.

---

1   What chore did Forrest like least?

a. emptying the prisoners' chamber pots
b. cleaning the ravens' cages
c. preparing the ravens' meals
d. clipping the ravens' wings

_____ Initials

---

2   Who brought Forrest and Rat together as friends?

a. Tuck
b. Simon Frick
c. The Ravenmaster
d. Mary and Bea

_____ Initials

---

3   What is meant when the Ravenmaster tells Forrest *"most climbing boys don't live to see their beards come in"*?

a. The climbing boys leave work to live in the city.
b. The climbing boys live to be old men.
c. The climbing boys die at a young age.

_____ Initials

---

4   Who visited Forrest and Rat at the shed?

a. Master Meeks
b. Simon Frick
c. The Ravenmaster
d. A Yeoman Warder

_____ Initials

---

5   With what offense were the Scottish Rebels charged?

a. conspiracy against the King
b. murder of a Yeoman Warder
c. treason
d. abandonment of country values

_____ Initials

---

6   What did Forrest and Rat imagine when they returned from seeing the prisoners being unloaded?

a. life in a large green field
b. the world beyond the Tower walls
c. swimming in the free ocean
d. running among the streets in the city

_____ Initials

---

7   Why did the Bloody Tower have an extra deep step?

a. to ward off the ghosts
b. to cause the guards to be careful
c. to stop those trying to escape
d. to prevent visitors from seeing prisoners

_____ Initials

---

8   What noise caused both boys to be frozen in fear?

a. Tuck's warning call
b. a haunting song
c. scraping of a prisoner door
d. footsteps from above

_____ Initials

---

9   What did Rat offer the young Scottish prisoner?

a. a warm blanket to sleep with
b. a glass of clean water
c. a ginger biscuit from Forrest
d. a hand to help her off the floor

_____ Initials

Cooperative Learning & Literature
Kagan Publishing • (800) 933-2667 • www.KaganOnline.com

Recall Questions

The Ravenmaster's Secret: Escape from the Tower of London • Chapers XII–XIV

Directions: Participate in Find Someone Who to answer the recall questions about *The Ravenmaster's Secret: Escape from the Tower of London.* Circle the correct answer provided by your partner and have your partner initial the answer.

1 What did Mary tend to complain about to get out of her chores?

a. sore back
b. headache
c. toothache
d. itchy feet

_____ Initials

2 What did Rat offer Forrest to help with the bullies?

a. a bag of dead rats
b. a good-luck nail
c. Tuck's protection
d. tips for hiding from the boys

_____ Initials

3 What did the young female prisoner ask Forrest on his second visit?

a. Why am I here?
b. What is your name?
c. What news of my father?
d. When do I get supper?

_____ Initials

4 How did Forrest know the prisoner's family must be very wealthy?

a. They bought better food.
b. Their gold was brought in from Scotland.
c. Their clothes were made of fine material.
d. They were least able to take care of themselves.

_____ Initials

5 What caused the color to drain from Maddy's face?

a. Rat's hands and clothes were dirty.
b. A large river rat came into her cell.
c. Forrest said she would be hung tomorrow.
d. She saw her father's ghost.

_____ Initials

6 What is Rat's real name?

a. Forrest
b. Ned
c. Simon
d. Whipley

_____ Initials

7 How did Maddy learn to speak English?

a. Her grandfather taught her.
b. She loved to listen to old English songs.
c. Her nurse, Flora, taught her.
d. Her father was from England.

_____ Initials

8 Why did Maddy believe Forrest was a spy?

a. He asked where she had been staying the past few weeks.
b. He wanted to know what crime she had committed.
c. He said he didn't know where her father was.
d. He wanted to know about her family.

_____ Initials

9 If you wanted to learn more about the Tower of London and the Yeoman Warders, where would you look?

a. encyclopedia
b. atlas
c. interview a guard
d. newspaper article

_____ Initials

Recall Questions
The Ravenmaster's Secret: Escape from the Tower of London • Chapters XV–XVII

Directions: Participate in Find Someone Who to answer the recall questions about *The Ravenmaster's Secret: Escape from the Tower of London*. Circle the correct answer provided by your partner and have your partner initial the answer.

1 Why did Forrest need to keep his shoes dry?

a. His mother would be mad.
b. He only had one pair of shoes.
c. He did not want to leave wet footprints.
d. He did not want to slip on the stone stairs in the towers.

_____ Initials

2 How did Forrest know the fourth child following Master Frick was Ned?

a. Ned called out to Forrest.
b. Master Frick whacked Ned on the head with his cane.
c. Forrest recognized Ned's blue cap.
d. Forrest was the smallest of the children.

_____ Initials

3 Why was Ned with Master Frick?

a. Ned was able to make more money as a chimney sweep.
b. Master Frick would be able to provide Ned with a better bed.
c. Master Meeks sold Ned in a card game.
d. Ned was caught stealing from Master Frick.

_____ Initials

4 Where did Maddy get a candle?

a. There was one left in the cell from the bishop.
b. Maddy's father sent it to her from home.
c. The Ravenmaster brought it to her with supper.
d. A priest gave it to her during his visit.

_____ Initials

5 Why was Maddy drawing on the floor with a piece of charcoal?

a. to ward off evil
b. to pass the hours sitting alone
c. to help her remember her family
d. to ask for forgiveness for her sins

_____ Initials

6 What does the inscription "dree yer ain weird" mean on Maddy's ring?

a. help your friends
b. face up to your destiny
c. honor your country
d. a mother's love

_____ Initials

7 For what reason was Maddy being held prisoner?

a. telling lies to the English army
b. speaking against the king
c. helping her father plot to kill the king
d. trying to put out the fire set to her family home

_____ Initials

8 What did Maddy offer Forrest in exchange for taking the rowan to her father?

a. a bag of gold coins
b. a ride to her homeland
c. her ruby ring
d. her velvet green cape

_____ Initials

9 What determines if a prisoner is hung or beheaded for his or her crimes?

a. gender
b. noble blood
c. location
d. citizenship

_____ Initials

Recall Questions

The Ravenmaster's Secret: Escape from the Tower of London • Chapters XVIII–XXII

Directions: Participate in Find Someone Who to answer the recall questions about *The Ravenmaster's Secret: Escape from the Tower of London*. Circle the correct answer provided by your partner and have your partner initial the answer.

1 How did Forrest get into the Rebel Scot's tower?

a. paid the guard a half pence
b. offered the warders his mother's pie
c. showed the new warder Tuck's tricks
d. pretended to be lost

_____ Initials

2 What did the smell of tallow and lye remind Forrest of?

a. It was wash day.
b. His mother planned to go to the market.
c. He needed to hurry to help Tuck.
d. It was bath day.

_____ Initials

3 What did Forrest discover when looking for the ring?

a. Rat's lucky nail
b. a baby feather from Tuck
c. a hole in his pocket
d. a gold coin

_____ Initials

4 What did Forrest tell Maddy the morning before her departure to Westminster?

a. He believed she was innocent.
b. She was the best friend he ever had.
c. He would never forget her.
d. He was sad he would not see her again.

_____ Initials

5 What did the Rebel Scots do on their way to Westminster?

a. killed the ship's captain
b. threw the warders overboard
c. jumped into the river and tried to swim away
d. sang songs to alert other Scots in the area

_____ Initials

6 Why was Simon Frick disappointed with Ned?

a. Ned was too large to fit up the chimneys.
b. Ned was afraid of the dark.
c. Ned had burnt his knees and his skin was too delicate.
d. Ned had run away.

_____ Initials

7 Who visited Forrest while he was feeding the birds?

a. the Ravenmaster
b. a carpenter
c. the Constable
d. Master Meeks

_____ Initials

8 What did Forrest learn from talking with the mysterious visitor?

a. Maddy had died on her way to Westminster.
b. Ned would be hung in the morning for stealing.
c. Maddy's trial had been denied and she's been sentenced to die by the axe.
d. The Rebel Scots had escaped.

_____ Initials

9 What role did Forrest play in Maddy's escape?

a. distract the guards
b. bring Maddy her supper
c. switch places with her at night
d. bring the female visitors to her cell

_____ Initials

Recall Questions

The Ravenmaster's Secret: Escape from the Tower of London • Chapters XXIII–XXIX

Directions: Participate in Find Someone Who to answer the recall questions about *The Ravenmaster's Secret: Escape from the Tower of London*. Circle the correct answer provided by your partner and have your partner initial the answer.

---

1 Who startled Forrest when he returned to the shed?

a. Ned
b. Tuck
c. Mistress Harper
d. Maddy

_____
Initials

---

2 Why was Forrest taking extra care with his family?

a. He would be running away in the morning.
b. He was afraid he might never see them again.
c. He knew he would be hung for treason by helping Maddy.
d. Forrest would never be able to return home.

_____
Initials

---

3 Why was Ned so willing to help Maddy escape?

a. He had never had a friend like her before.
b. Ned knew his life wasn't worth much with the sweep after him.
c. Ned wanted to be sure he would be remembered for doing good.
d. Forrest always thought it was best to help others first.

_____
Initials

---

4 What did Forrest tell the warders about why Ned was with him?

a. Ned wanted to meet a Scottish lassie.
b. Forrest needed Ned to carry the thrush.
c. Ned needed to catch a rat.
d. Maddy wanted a friend to stay with her during the night.

_____
Initials

---

5 Which of the following is NOT something Maddy did to escape?

a. trim her nails
b. switch clothes with Ned
c. cut her hair
d. cover her face in ash

_____
Initials

---

6 What did Ned make Forrest promise before leaving the Tower?

a. never to forget his friendship
b. not to let them hang him in a dress
c. apologize to Simon Frick for running away
d. teach Tuck to say Ned

_____
Initials

---

7 Where did Maddy hide when Forrest went back for Ned?

a. in Master Meek's basement
b. with Tuck in the rafters
c. in an empty barrel
d. under some straw

_____
Initials

---

8 What new trick did Tuck perform for the warders?

a. flew upside down
b. said *"King George"*
c. played keep away with the warder's hat
d. sang England's national anthem

_____
Initials

---

9 What did Forrest request to do once he returned home?

a. sleep with his sister Bea
b. fix Tuck a special dinner
c. look for Ned
d. sleep in the shed

_____
Initials

Recall Questions

The Ravenmaster's Secret: Escape from the Tower of London • Chapters XXX–Epilogue

Directions: Participate in Find Someone Who to answer the recall questions about *The Ravenmaster's Secret: Escape from the Tower of London*. Circle the correct answer provided by your partner and have your partner initial the answer.

1 Who did Ned encounter on his way to find Maddy and Forrest?
a. Tuck
b. the priest helping Maddy
c. Simon Frick
d. Master Meeks

Initials

2 Who caught Maddy, Ned, and Forrest during the escape?
a. Ravenmaster Harper
b. Simon Frick
c. Master Meeks
d. the Constable

Initials

3 Which of the following is NOT a reason Forrest stayed behind?
a. His home was in the Tower.
b. His father expected him to be Ravenmaster one day.
c. He could not leave Tuck behind.
d. He did not want to leave his family.

Initials

4 What did Forrest give to Ned before he departed?
a. Tuck's feather
b. the lucky bent nail
c. Maddy's ring
d. the spyglass

Initials

5 Who was blamed for Maddy's escape?
a. Ned
b. Forrest
c. Simon Frick
d. Tuck

Initials

6 To whom did Forrest tell his secret about Maddy's escape?
a. his father
b. Simon Frick
c. no one
d. his daughter

Initials

7 What is meant by the phrase, "thirty springs had come and gone"?
a. The rivers are still flowing.
b. Thirty years have passed in the story.
c. The story is going into the past by thirty years.
d. Forrest is thirty years old.

Initials

8 Where did Ned go after leaving with Maddy?
a. home to London
b. to find his parents
c. work on a whaling ship
d. to the Glenn with Maddy

Initials

9 What did Forrest receive with Ned's letter?
a. the spyglass
b. pictures from the sea
c. a letter from Maddy
d. a map of all of his travels

Initials

Recall Questions
The Ravenmaster's Secret: Escape from the Tower of London

Directions: Participate in Find Someone Who to answer the recall questions about *The Ravenmaster's Secret: Escape from the Tower of London*. Write the answer in the space provided. Have your partner initial the answer.

1 Who are three of the main characters?

_____
_____
_____
_____
Initials

2 What was the nickname Forrest received on collar day?

_____
_____
_____
_____
Initials

3 List two chores Forrest had to do each day.

_____
_____
_____
_____
Initials

4 What was Rat's real name?

_____
_____
_____
_____
Initials

5 What did the inscription on Maddy's ring say?

_____
_____
_____
_____
Initials

6 Where does the story take place?

_____
_____
_____
_____
Initials

7 What was the name of Forrests' raven?

_____
_____
_____
_____
Initials

8 Who was blamed for Maddy's prison escape?

_____
_____
_____
_____
Initials

9 What was the charge against Maddy?

_____
_____
_____
_____
Initials

10 Why did Maddy's original escape plan fail?

_____
_____
_____
_____
Initials

11 Who won Rat's indenture during a card game with Master Meeks?

_____
_____
_____
_____
Initials

12 What did Ned send to Forrest (Ravenmaster Harper) years later after his escape?

_____
_____
_____
_____
Initials

Cooperative Learning & Literature
Kagan Publishing • (800) 933-2667 • www.KaganOnline.com

Journal Writing

The Ravenmaster's Secret: Escape from the Tower of London • "By the Scaffold Steps"

Directions: Think about the Journal Question, and then write your own response. When done, RoundRobin share your writing with your teammates. Use the space at the bottom to record ideas your teammates share.

Journal Question
Evaluate London's reaction to a hanging. What do you feel about the people's behavior? Was this normal for the time period?

Journal Response: _____

_____

_____

_____

_____

_____

_____

_____

_____

_____

Ideas Teammates Shared

Journal Writing

The Ravenmaster's Secret: Escape from the Tower of London • "Through the Spyglass"

Directions: Think about the Journal Question, and then write your own response. When done, RoundRobin share your writing with your teammates. Use the space at the bottom to record ideas your teammates share.

Journal Question
Forrest and Rat imagine themselves on a ship exploring the world.
Is this a dream that could happen for them? Explain.

Journal Response: _____

_____

_____

_____

_____

_____

_____

_____

_____

_____

_____

Ideas Teammates Shared

Cooperative Learning & Literature
Kagan Publishing • (800) 933-2667 • www.KaganOnline.com

Journal Writing

The Ravenmaster's Secret: Escape from the Tower of London • "The Fourth Shadow"

Directions: Think about the Journal Question, and then write your own response. When done, RoundRobin share your writing with your teammates. Use the space at the bottom to record ideas your teammates share.

Journal Question

Why did Rat have to work for Simon Frick? Research child slaves and workers from the past. How is Rat's situation similar to other kids through history?

Journal Response: _____

_____

_____

_____

_____

_____

_____

_____

_____

_____

_____

Ideas Teammates Shared

Journal Writing

The Ravenmaster's Secret: Escape from the Tower of London • "For Her Eyes Only"

Directions: Think about the Journal Question, and then write your own response. When done, RoundRobin share your writing with your teammates. Use the space at the bottom to record ideas your teammates share.

Journal Question
Make a prediction about what will happen with Maddy's future?

Journal Response: _____

_____

_____

_____

_____

_____

_____

_____

_____

_____

_____

Ideas Teammates Shared

Cooperative Learning & Literature
Kagan Publishing • (800) 933-2667 • www.KaganOnline.com

Journal Writing

The Ravenmaster's Secret: Escape from the Tower of London • "Out of Luck"

Directions: Think about the Journal Question, and then write your own response. When done, RoundRobin share your writing with your teammates. Use the space at the bottom to record ideas your teammates share.

Journal Question
How does the Ravenmaster's story of Odin and Henry compare to Maddy and Forrest? How does the story help Forrest with his decisions? Explain and justify.

Journal Response: _____

_____

_____

_____

_____

_____

_____

_____

_____

_____

_____

_____

Ideas Teammates Shared

Journal Writing

The Ravenmaster's Secret: Escape from the Tower of London • "A Dirty Lie"

Directions: Think about the Journal Question, and then write your own response. When done, RoundRobin share your writing with your teammates. Use the space at the bottom to record ideas your teammates share.

Journal Question
How do the chapter titles reflect what happens in the chapters?
Does the reader know the meanings at the beginning of the chapter or the end? Explain.

Journal Response: _____

_____

_____

_____

_____

_____

_____

_____

_____

_____

_____

Ideas Teammates Shared

Cooperative Learning & Literature
Kagan Publishing • (800) 933-2667 • www.KaganOnline.com

Journal Writing

The Ravenmaster's Secret: Escape from the Tower of London • End-of-Book

Directions: Think about the Journal Question, and then write your own response. When done, RoundRobin share your writing with your teammates. Use the space at the bottom to record ideas your teammates share.

Journal Question
How does the adventure of Maddy's escape affect Forrest later in life? Explain.

Journal Response: _____

_____

_____

_____

_____

_____

_____

_____

_____

_____

_____

_____

Ideas Teammates Shared

Journal Writing

The Ravenmaster's Secret: Escape from the Tower of London • End-of-Book

Directions: Think about the Journal Question, and then write your own response. When done, RoundRobin share your writing with your teammates. Use the space at the bottom to record ideas your teammates share.

Journal Question

This story takes place at the Tower of London and is historical fiction, which means the author based the story on real facts. What parts of the story are probably real and what parts are made up by the author?

Journal Response: _____

_____

_____

_____

_____

_____

_____

_____

_____

_____

Ideas Teammates Shared

Higher-Level Thinking Cards
The Ravenmaster's Secret: Escape from the Tower of London

Directions: Copy enough cards so that each student receives a Question Card. Have students stand up, pair up, and do Traveling Pair Share to respond to each other's questions. Students trade cards and find a new partner to share.

---

1 — The Ravenmaster's Secret: Escape from the Tower of London

What was Rat's job at the beginning of the story? Describe how Rat's job affected the story.

Traveling Pair Share

---

2 — The Ravenmaster's Secret: Escape from the Tower of London

How would you have solved Rat's problem? Do you think it would have worked?

Traveling Pair Share

---

3 — The Ravenmaster's Secret: Escape from the Tower of London

What observations did you make about Forrest?

Traveling Pair Share

---

4 — The Ravenmaster's Secret: Escape from the Tower of London

How are you alike or different from Maddy? Forrest? Rat?

Traveling Pair Share

---

5 — The Ravenmaster's Secret: Escape from the Tower of London

What part of the story might you eliminate? Why?

Traveling Pair Share

---

6 — The Ravenmaster's Secret: Escape from the Tower of London

What is your opinion of the story? Use details in your answer.

Traveling Pair Share

---

7 — The Ravenmaster's Secret: Escape from the Tower of London

What symbol would you say represents the story? Why did you choose this symbol?

Traveling Pair Share

---

8 — The Ravenmaster's Secret: Escape from the Tower of London

How did Forrest change from the beginning of the story to the end?

Traveling Pair Share

Higher-Level Thinking Cards
The Ravenmaster's Secret: Escape from the Tower of London

Directions: Copy enough cards so that each student receives a Question Card. Have students stand up, pair up, and do Traveling Pair Share to respond to each other's questions. Students trade cards and find a new partner to share.

---

(9) The Ravenmaster's Secret: Escape from the Tower of London

What is your favorite part of the story? Why?

Traveling Pair Share

---

(10) The Ravenmaster's Secret: Escape from the Tower of London

How would you explain Rat's indenture?

Traveling Pair Share

---

(11) The Ravenmaster's Secret: Escape from the Tower of London

How would you feel if you were in Maddy's shoes?

Traveling Pair Share

---

(12) The Ravenmaster's Secret: Escape from the Tower of London

Do you agree or disagree with Maddy's punishment? Explain.

Traveling Pair Share

---

(13) The Ravenmaster's Secret: Escape from the Tower of London

What feelings did you have while reading *The Ravenmaster's Secret: Escape from the Tower of London?* Explain your reactions.

Traveling Pair Share

---

(14) The Ravenmaster's Secret: Escape from the Tower of London

How did Maddy and Forrest's friendship change during the story?

Traveling Pair Share

---

(15) The Ravenmaster's Secret: Escape from the Tower of London

Would you like to go back into time and visit the Tower of London? Why or why not?

Traveling Pair Share

---

(16) The Ravenmaster's Secret: Escape from the Tower of London

Which character would you like to meet the most: Forrest, Maddy or Ned? Explain.

Traveling Pair Share

Cooperative Learning & Literature
Kagan Publishing • (800) 933-2667 • www.KaganOnline.com

Stuart Little

By E. B. White

The Little family is surprised when their second child Stuart turns out to be no larger than a mouse, and remarkably similar, complete with a tail and whiskers. There are dangers of being a mouse so small and trying to fit in with human life. Cats, stray dogs, garbage cans, mouse holes, and much more become huge obstacles. However, a lot of fun can be found as well, such as sailboat racing on the open waters or driving an invisible car! During Stuart's adventures, he finds some unique friends and overcomes difficult challenges. This is a story about one small being who finds grand adventures in a large world.

Reading Level

Lexile Level: 920L
Guided Reading Level: R
DRA Level: 40
Accelerated Reader: 3.9

Stuart Little

~ Cooperative Learning Activities ~

Cooperative Learning & Literature
Kagan Publishing • (800) 933-2667 • www.KaganOnline.com

Recall Questions
Stuart Little • Chapters 1–3

Directions: Participate in Find Someone Who to answer the recall questions about *Stuart Little*. Circle the correct answer provided by your partner and have your partner initial the answer.

1 Where does the story *Stuart Little* take place?
a. England
b. New York City
c. Boston
d. California
_____ Initials

2 How did Stuart assist Mrs. Little in finding her lost ring?
a. Stuart crawled under the sink.
b. Stuart told Mr. Little about it.
c. Stuart went down the bathtub drain.
d. Stuart helped George look under the bathroom floorboards.
_____ Initials

3 Why did Stuart need to sprinkle himself with a bit of violet water?
a. He was covered in dust from the sofa.
b. He just finished doing his exercises.
c. He wanted to smell fresh and clean.
d. He felt slimy and dirty.
_____ Initials

4 What caused Stuart to have perspiration rolling down his cheeks?
a. He was working hard rolling ping-pong balls.
b. He had finished running a race.
c. He was tired from climbing the stairs.
d. He played baseball with George.
_____ Initials

5 Why did Stuart find the piano exciting?
a. The hammers were fun to jump.
b. George liked to sing along as he played.
c. The music was quite terrific.
d. The inside of a piano is like a maze.
_____ Initials

6 What did Mr. Little request his wife do about having a mouse in the family?
a. cover all mouse holes
b. keep Stuart off the counters
c. allow him to be just like George
d. not to reference mice in their conversations
_____ Initials

7 Why did the mouse hole worry Mr. Little?
a. He knew a big rat lived there.
b. The wires in the walls were dangerous.
c. He didn't know where the hole led to.
d. The walls were not safe for a mouse.
_____ Initials

8 How was Stuart able to turn the light on in the bathroom?
a. He has a special stomp pad to jump on.
b. He shinnied up the wall.
c. He waited until Mr. Little woke up.
d. He pulled a long string attached to the pull-chain of the light.
_____ Initials

9 Which statement best describes George?
a. George is easily distracted and leaves things unfinished.
b. George loves having a mouse as a pet.
c. George is very spoiled.
d. George pays close attention to details.
_____ Initials

10 What did Stuart use to turn the faucet to get water?
a. a piece of rope
b. a large piece of wood
c. a small hammer
d. his little mouse hands
_____ Initials

11 Which could be another title for Chapter 3 "Washing Up"?
a. "Taking a Bath"
b. "Morning Routine"
c. "Hard Tasks for George"
d. "Family Love"
_____ Initials

12 Which of the following would Stuart be able to do successfully?
a. go bowling
b. vacuum the house
c. cook dinner
d. gather small beads on the ground
_____ Initials

Recall Questions
Stuart Little • Chapters 4–6

Directions: Participate in Find Someone Who to answer the recall questions about *Stuart Little*. Circle the correct answer provided by your partner and have your partner initial the answer.

1 What was the result of Stuart showing off his muscles?
a. He pulled a muscle and had to go to bed.
b. He got pulled up and wrapped into the window shade.
c. He was told to be quiet.
d. Snowbell pushed him off the table.
_____ Initials

2 What did Snowbell do after Stuart was trapped?
a. ran to find Mrs. Little
b. shut the door and went outside
c. helped Stuart become free
d. placed Stuart's cane and hat near a mousehole
_____ Initials

3 In what ways did George try to help Stuart?
a. created missing person flyers
b. called the police and ambulance
c. drove to the nearest hospital
d. poured applesauce into the hole
_____ Initials

4 What was George's reason for pulling down the shade?
a. to respect the dead
b. to look for Stuart
c. it was getting dark
d. to prevent Snowbell from looking outside
_____ Initials

5 Where did Stuart hide if he spied a dog?
a. in the garbage can
b. behind a lamppost
c. up a doorman's trousers
d. inside a mailbox
_____ Initials

6 What was actually one of Stuart's dimes?
a. a plastic penny
b. a piece of tin foil
c. a doll prop
d. a shaving from Mr. Little's dime
_____ Initials

7 What was the name of the boat Stuart admired?
a. *Wasp*
b. *Schooner*
c. *Fair Maiden*
d. *Clipper*
_____ Initials

8 Why did the man allow Stuart to sail?
a. The winds were very strong.
b. The man wanted to beat another boat.
c. Stuart was known as a fine sailor.
d. The man needed someone very small.
_____ Initials

9 What was Mrs. Little's reason for wanting to call out to Stuart?
a. Stuart had very poor hearing and they needed to shout.
b. Mrs. Little was worried Stuart was afraid of the dark.
c. Mrs. Little thought Stuart might have lost his way.
d. Mr. Little was frightened the rats would find Stuart.
_____ Initials

10 Which title could best replace the title of Chapter 5, "Rescued"?
a. "Stuart Lost and Found"
b. "Danger Avoided"
c. "Snowbell Eats Stuart"
d. "Small Spaces"
_____ Initials

11 Which question is answered in Chapters 4–6?
a. Will Snowbell and Stuart ever become friends?
b. Is Stuart able to sail a small boat?
c. What will Stuart be when he grows up?
d. Who is Stuart's best friend?
_____ Initials

12 If you wanted to learn more about the meaning of the words "jib, squall, deck, and mast," where would you look?
a. encyclopedia
b. *Stuart Little*
c. atlas
d. dictionary
_____ Initials

Recall Questions
Stuart Little • Chapters 7–8

Directions: Participate in Find Someone Who to answer the recall questions about *Stuart Little*. Circle the correct answer provided by your partner and have your partner initial the answer.

1 What was the result of Stuart sailing a ship?
a. Stuart got seasick.
b. Everyone ran from the lake.
c. A large crowd formed to watch.
d. Stuart was asked to pose for pictures.
Initials

2 How did LeRoy try to get Stuart to steer his boat instead?
a. threatened to tell the police that Stuart did not have a license
b. offered to pay Stuart $5 a week
c. gave Stuart his own captian's hat
d. named the boat *The Stuart*
Initials

3 What caused the policeman to end up in the water?
a. The policeman tried to rescue a drowning boy.
b. The policeman needed to stop LeRoy from sinking the boat.
c. The people were pushing each other to see the race.
d. The people threw him in when he said they had to leave.
Initials

4 What trouble did the barometer suggest?
a. windy seas
b. approaching boats
c. high waves
d. stormy weather
Initials

5 What object caused Stuart problems during the storm?
a. captain's hat
b. torn sail
c. paper bag
d. broken paddle
Initials

6 Why did the policeman not shake hands with Stuart?
a. Stuart was too small.
b. He was too wet and mad.
c. He refused to touch a mouse.
d. Stuart had already left.
Initials

7 What was the reason Mr. Little made Stuart a tiny red cap?
a. Stuart could never reach the TV.
b. Stuart was often hard to find around the house.
c. Stuart had trouble riding a bike.
d. Stuart could not go swimming.
Initials

8 What caused Stuart to get bronchitis?
a. forgetting his hat at home
b. trying to walk in the snow
c. spending the night in the rain
d. being trapped in the refrigerator
Initials

9 What prevented Snowbell from attacking Margalo?
a. Stuart shot Snowbell with an arrow.
b. Margalo flew out of reach.
c. Mrs. Little came into the room.
d. George locked Snowbell outside the house.
Initials

10 What was a result of Stuart being sick?
a. The family was extremely kind to Stuart.
b. Mrs. Little put a bell inside the refrigerator.
c. Stuart's friends came to visit him.
d. Mr. Little gave him a hot bath.
Initials

11 How did Stuart know Margalo's temperature was normal?
a. Stuart felt Margalo's head.
b. Stuart asked Mrs. Little.
c. Margalo used a thermometer.
d. Stuart's feet were not cold.
Initials

12 Which question can be answered after reading Chapter 8?
a. What kind of bird is Margalo?
b. Where was Stuart born?
c. Will Snowbell try to attack Margalo?
d. Will Stuart and Margalo become friends?
Initials

Recall Questions
Stuart Little • Chapters 9–10

Directions: Participate in Find Someone Who to answer the recall questions about *Stuart Little*. Circle the correct answer provided by your partner and have your partner initial the answer.

1 Which pair of words best describes Stuart's time in the garbage?
a. exciting and thrilling
b. dark and dry
c. anxious and scary
d. relaxing and soothing
_____ Initials

2 Which phrase is most likely the meaning of the word "scow" found in Chapter 9?
a. a flat bed truck
b. submarine
c. type of boat
d. game played in water
_____ Initials

3 Where were Stuart and the trash headed?
a. an underground dump
b. the Atlantic Ocean
c. a cave off shore
d. a large farm field
_____ Initials

4 What was the solution for Stuart being taken out with the garbage?
a. Stuart jumped in the water.
b. Margalo carried him back home.
c. George stopped the garbage man.
d. Stuart called the rescue squad.
_____ Initials

5 What did Margalo ask Stuart to do to make him lighter?
a. stop eating so many cookies
b. drop his paperclip ice skates
c. remove his coat and hat
d. hang on only by his tail
_____ Initials

6 How did Mrs. Little reward Margalo?
a. Mrs. Little created a special sleeping pillow for her.
b. Mrs. Little presented her with a cake sprinkled with seeds.
c. She allowed Margalo to sit at the table.
d. She gave Margalo a new climbing rope.
_____ Initials

7 What is the result of Snowbell holding himself in as a cat?
a. He was terribly nervous and upset.
b. He craved bird stew for dinner.
c. He was growing fat and lazy.
d. His cat friends did not want to play with him anymore.
_____ Initials

8 What conclusion can you make about Snowbell?
a. He really cares for Stuart and Maraglo.
b. He does not care if someone else eats Margalo.
c. He is protective of his family.
d. He does not like the taste of birds.
_____ Initials

9 What was Margalo's solution to her problem?
a. She asked Stuart for help.
b. She asked George to put her into a cage for the night.
c. She asked Mrs. Little to lock all of the windows and doors.
d. She decided to fly north.
_____ Initials

10 How did Margalo learn about the strange cat's plan?
a. She overheard his converstation from the window.
b. Snowbell told Stuart after dinner.
c. A pigeon left a note for Margalo.
d. Mrs. Little knew the cats were up to trouble.
_____ Initials

11 Who is telling the story of *Stuart Little*?
a. Snowbell
b. George
c. the narrator
d. Mr. Little
_____ Initials

12 What was Snowbell's reason for not eating the bird and mouse?
a. Stuart is a member of the family, and the bird is a permanent guest.
b. Snowbell prefers cat food to birds and mice.
c. Snowbell did not want to upset George.
d. Stuart was too smart for Snowbell.
_____ Initials

Cooperative Learning & Literature
Kagan Publishing • (800) 933-2667 • www.KaganOnline.com

Recall Questions
Stuart Little • Chapters 11–12

Directions: Participate in Find Someone Who to answer the recall questions about *Stuart Little*. Circle the correct answer provided by your partner and have your partner initial the answer.

1 What was the effect of Margalo's disappearance on Stuart?
a. Stuart refused to eat and lost weight.
b. Stuart stayed in bed all day.
c. Stuart walked down the street and looked in every tree.
d. Stuart started to make missing posters.
_____ Initials

2 What item did Stuart take to remember his mother before leaving?
a. a large-toothed comb
b. a strand of hair
c. a miniature picture
d. a small eyelash
_____ Initials

3 Who did Stuart decide to find to ask for advice?
a. Margalo
b. Snowbell
c. Dr. Carey
d. a long-lost friend
_____ Initials

4 What was the author's reasoning for writing the sentence, "How 'oo oo, Soo'rt?
a. to show that Stuart was whispering
b. to challenge the reader
c. to demonstrate the man talking with gauze in his cheek
d. to teach the reader not to talk with his or her mouth full
_____ Initials

5 What was special about the toy automobile Dr. Carey gave to Stuart?
a. It was made by a gypsy.
b. It had a real gasoline motor.
c. It was painted green and brown.
d. It was Dr. Carey's favorite car to drive.
_____ Initials

6 Why was the man on the side of the road sad?
a. The car had broken down and he was late for work.
b. He missed the bus to work.
c. One of his teachers was sick.
d. He could not find his missing briefcase.
_____ Initials

7 What was Stuart's plan to maintain discipline while at the school?
a. be strict and unkind
b. make the learning interesting
c. give a lot of homework
d. play games and have fun
_____ Initials

8 What subject did Stuart suggest the scholars discuss?
a. Arithmetic
b. Reading
c. World History
d. King of the World
_____ Initials

9 What advice did Stuart give the scholars before leaving?
a. Never forget your summertimes.
b. Read every night for several hours.
c. Learn to love school.
d. Follow your dreams and reach for the stars.
_____ Initials

10 What reason did Mrs. Little give for Margalo's disappearance?
a. Margalo might have a husband somewhere.
b. Margalo was homesick.
c. Snowbell had eaten Margalo.
d. Margalo needed space to fly.
_____ Initials

11 What did Dr. Carey tell Stuart before leaving?
a. Be sure to drive the back roads.
b. Do not go too fast.
c. Never push a button on an automobile unless you know what you are doing.
_____ Initials

12 What did Stuart do to prepare to be the substitute teacher?
a. read the lesson plans
b. changed into a suit
c. called the parents
d. prepared a video
_____ Initials

Recall Questions
Stuart Little • Chapters 13–15

Directions: Participate in Find Someone Who to answer the recall questions about *Stuart Little*. Circle the correct answer provided by your partner and have your partner initial the answer.

1 What conclusion can you make about Harriet Ames?
a. Harriet was born into a well-known family.
b. Harriet does not like being so small.
c. Harriet likes to walk around town.
d. Harriet's family is ashamed of their daughter.
_____ Initials

2 What made Stuart almost fall into the ink well?
a. The door slamming scared him.
b. The postmaster set a box on the table.
c. A girl about two-inches high entered the room.
d. Stuart slipped off the rim.
_____ Initials

3 What was the reason Stuart wrote a letter to Miss Ames?
a. to invite her to a party
b. to ask her to go for a paddle in a canoe
c. to ask her where she was born
d. to tell her he would like to visit her at her house
_____ Initials

4 What did Stuart ask for at the store?
a. a stamp to mail the letter
b. a small writing utensil
c. a canoe and paddle
d. a set of roller skates
_____ Initials

5 How did Stuart get the canoe to the water?
a. attached it to his automobile
b. asked the storekeeper to deliver it
c. carried it over his head
d. Dr. Carey attached it to his favorite car.
_____ Initials

6 Why was Stuart upset when he got to the water?
a. It was raining.
b. He discovered he had been swindled.
c. The river was overflowing.
d. His campsite had been destroyed.
_____ Initials

7 Why did Stuart chop down the dandelion with an ax?
a. to give Harriet a flower as a present
b. to create a hammock
c. to drink the milk
d. to use the peddles for a rug
_____ Initials

8 Why was Stuart brokenhearted when he reached the canoe?
a. It had sunk to the bottom of river.
b. It was a mess after some big boys had played with it.
c. The paddles had crumbled.
d. Harriet refused to get in the canoe.
_____ Initials

9 What did Stuart do following his time with Harriet?
a. returned home to the Littles'
b. went with Harriet to her house
c. canoed on down the river
d. continued his journey north
_____ Initials

10 What genre is the story of *Stuart Little*?
a. realistic fiction
b. biography
c. fairy tale
d. fantasy
_____ Initials

11 Which question can be answered after reading *Stuart Little*?
a. Will Stuart ever find Margalo?
b. Is Stuart Little able to talk to humans?
c. Does Stuart return to live with the Littles again?
d. Who does Stuart marry?
_____ Initials

12 If you wanted to learn more about the author, E. B. White, what would be the best resource?
a. write a letter to the librarian
b. ask your parents for information
c. look up information on the Internet
d. read more books by E. B. White
_____ Initials

Cooperative Learning & Literature
Kagan Publishing • (800) 933-2667 • www.KaganOnline.com

Recall Questions
Stuart Little • End-of-Book

Directions: Copy one set of cards for each team. Cut out each card along the dotted line. Give each team a set of cards to play Fan-N-Pick or Showdown.

① Stuart Little

Why did Stuart go down the bath drain?

Fan-N-Pick/Showdown

② Stuart Little

What made the Littles believe Stuart had gone into the mousehole?

Fan-N-Pick/Showdown

③ Stuart Little

What item caused Stuart great trouble while out sailing the *Wasp*?

Fan-N-Pick/Showdown

④ Stuart Little

How did Stuart stop Snowbell from attacking Margalo?

Fan-N-Pick/Showdown

⑤ Stuart Little

How was Stuart saved from the garbage scow and from being dumped into the Atlantic Ocean?

Fan-N-Pick/Showdown

⑥ Stuart Little

What was special about the automobile Dr. Carey gave to Stuart?

Fan-N-Pick/Showdown

⑦ Stuart Little

How did Stuart help the Superintendent?

Fan-N-Pick/Showdown

⑧ Stuart Little

What made Stuart upset during his date with Harriet?

Fan-N-Pick/Showdown

Recall Questions
Stuart Little • End-of-Book

Directions: Copy one set of cards for each team. Cut out each card along the dotted line. Give each team a set of cards to play Fan-N-Pick or Showdown.

---

⑨ Stuart Little

What did Stuart do after talking to the telephone repairman?

Fan-N-Pick/Showdown

---

⑩ Stuart Little

How did Stuart help George when he practiced the piano?

Fan-N-Pick/Showdown

---

⑪ Stuart Little

What happened after Stuart tried to show his muscles to Snowbell?

Fan-N-Pick/Showdown

---

⑫ Stuart Little

What happened after Stuart was locked inside the cold refrigerator?

Fan-N-Pick/Showdown

---

⑬ Stuart Little

Where did Stuart seek shelter from the dog?

Fan-N-Pick/Showdown

---

⑭ Stuart Little

How did Stuart react when Margalo disappeared?

Fan-N-Pick/Showdown

---

⑮ Stuart Little

Which way did Stuart travel at the end of the book?

Fan-N-Pick/Showdown

---

⑯ Stuart Little

What did Mr. Little use to make Stuart's bed?

Fan-N-Pick/Showdown

Cooperative Learning & Literature
Kagan Publishing • (800) 933-2667 • www.KaganOnline.com

Journal Writing
Stuart Little • Chapter 2

Directions: Think about the Journal Question, and then write your own response. When done, RoundRobin share your writing with your teammates. Use the space at the bottom to record ideas your teammates share.

Journal Question
Should the Littles ask Stuart to help them out with special tasks around the house such as getting a ring from a drain or retrieving ping-pong balls from under the radiator? Explain your thinking.

Journal Response: _____

_____

_____

_____

_____

_____

_____

_____

_____

_____

_____

Ideas Teammates Shared

Journal Writing
Stuart Little • Chapter 4

Directions: Think about the Journal Question, and then write your own response. When done, RoundRobin share your writing with your teammates. Use the space at the bottom to record ideas your teammates share.

Journal Question
Is Stuart more like a mouse or more like a human? Explain.

Journal Response: _____

_____

_____

_____

_____

_____

_____

_____

_____

_____

_____

Ideas Teammates Shared

Journal Writing
Stuart Little • Chapter 6

Directions: Think about the Journal Question, and then write your own response. When done, RoundRobin share your writing with your teammates. Use the space at the bottom to record ideas your teammates share.

Journal Question
How did Stuart's feelings change throughout the chapter, "A Fair Breeze"?

Journal Response: _____

_____

_____

_____

_____

_____

_____

_____

_____

_____

_____

_____

Ideas Teammates Shared

Journal Writing
Stuart Little • Chapter 7

Directions: Think about the Journal Question, and then write your own response. When done, RoundRobin share your writing with your teammates. Use the space at the bottom to record ideas your teammates share.

Journal Question
Was Stuart a good substitute teacher? Would yo want Stuart to be a substitute teacher in your classroom? Explain your thinking.

Journal Response: _____

_____

_____

_____

_____

_____

_____

_____

_____

_____

Ideas Teammates Shared

Journal Writing
Stuart Little • Chapter 15

Directions: Think about the Journal Question, and then write your own response. When done, RoundRobin share your writing with your teammates. Use the space at the bottom to record ideas your teammates share.

Journal Question
What do you think about Stuart's reaction to his ruined plans?
Should he have done something differently?

Journal Response: _____

_____

_____

_____

_____

_____

_____

_____

_____

_____

_____

Ideas Teammates Shared

Journal Writing
Stuart Little • End-of-Book

Directions: Think about the Journal Question, and then write your own response. When done, RoundRobin share your writing with your teammates. Use the space at the bottom to record ideas your teammates share.

Journal Question
Imagine the author wrote another chapter about Stuart Little.
What would the author write about? Give the chapter a title.

Journal Response: _____

_____

_____

_____

_____

_____

_____

_____

_____

_____

_____

_____

Ideas Teammates Shared

Cooperative Learning & Literature
Kagan Publishing • (800) 933-2667 • www.KaganOnline.com

The Whipping Boy

By Sid Fleischman

A story set in the past when princes had royal whipping boys, we meet a common boy named Jemmy who once made a living catching rats in the sewer. He is now living in the King's castle as a whipping boy for Prince Brat and he dreams of running away. The Prince and his whipping boy start off as enemies but find they must depend on each other to escape from ruthless kidnappers who are planning to make a profit from the King. They encounter many obstacles while trying to escape. Once they are free and back at the castle, they become friends. Prince Brat learns to appreciate Jemmy's abilities and courage and vows to be a true friend to Jemmy and quit his selfish and spoiled ways.

Reading Level

Lexile Level: 570
Guided Reading Level: R
DRA Level: 40
Accelerated Reader: 3.9

The Whipping Boy

~ Cooperative Learning Activities ~

Recall Questions
The Whipping Boy • Chapters 1–6

❏ **RallyCoach Directions:** Take turns answering each question as your partner coaches. Explain your thinking to your coach.

❏ **Sage-N-Scribe Directions:** The Sage describes what he or she knows about the question so the Scribe can answer the question. The Sage and Scribe switch roles for each question.

Name _____

1. What did the Prince do one night during the King's grand feast?
   a. switched out the turkey for dog food
   b. tied the guests' wigs to their chairs
   c. threw a tantrum about not having dessert
   d. refused to shake hands with his guests

2. Why did the Prince not care that he couldn't write his name?
   a. He didn't plan on being a king.
   b. He wanted to make his tutor mad.
   c. He could always have his whipping boy read.
   d. He would have someone else write his name for him.

3. Why did Prince Brat request a manservant?
   a. He wanted to take a horse for a ride.
   b. He planned to run away.
   c. He was afraid to go to town alone.
   d. He needed help with his homework.

4. What caused Hold-Your-Nose Billy and Cutwater to think they caught a prince?
   a. The Prince sang the royal song.
   b. Jemmy was wearing the royal colors.
   c. The horse was wearing the King's crest.
   d. The horse was well taken care of with a jeweled bridle.

5. What did Cutwater find deeper in the Prince's basket?
   a. a letter from the King
   b. a bag of jewels
   c. a golden crown
   d. a horse's whip

Name _____

1. What was the King's request after Prince Brat disrupted the feast?
   a. Prince Brat would go to his room without food.
   b. All the Lords and Ladies should ignore the prince.
   c. The whipping boy shall get twenty whacks.
   d. The prince will get whipped for his behavior.

2. What did the whipping boy learn during his first year with the Prince?
   a. to read, write, and do sums
   b. to stay away from the Prince in the morning
   c. to ride a horse
   d. how to catch rats

3. Why was it difficult to travel after the Prince and Jemmy left the castle?
   a. People kept recognizing the Prince.
   b. The Prince refused to ride the horse alone.
   c. The fog made it difficult to see.
   d. The horse didn't want to leave the stables.

4. What did Hold-Your-Nose- Billy offer the boys to eat?
   a. bread and herring
   b. fruit tart and roasted pheasant
   c. stale bread and water
   d. rat meat

5. What decision did the outlaws make regarding the boys?
   a. sell the boys for gold to the highest bidder
   b. return the Prince for a reward and then keep the whipping boy
   c. write a letter to the King demanding 55 pounds of gold
   d. make them help rob others on the road

Recall Questions
The Whipping Boy • Chapters 7–14

❑ **RallyCoach Directions:** Take turns answering each question as your partner coaches. Explain your thinking to your coach.

❑ **Sage-N-Scribe Directions:** The Sage describes what he or she knows about the question so the Scribe can answer the question. The Sage and Scribe switch roles for each question.

Name _____

1. What does the underlined word mean in this sentence? "I'm thinking these lads have mixed themselves up to <u>flummox</u> us."
 a. confuse
 b. make fools of
 c. play a trick on
 d. excite

2. What word best describes how Prince Brat was feeling after Jemmy said he was the Prince?
 a. delighted
 b. jealous
 c. confused
 d. angry

3. What was Jemmy's first suggestion for delivering the note to the King?
 a. Jemmy's whipping boy could take it.
 b. Jemmy would deliver the note by hand.
 c. Hold-Your-Nose-Billy should take it.
 d. Give the note to the nearest royal messenger.

4. Why would the King NOT pay the ransom of a wagon full of gold and jewels?
 a. The King did not own jewels.
 b. The Prince was a brat.
 c. The King would know the Prince did not write the message.
 d. Jemmy had told the King not to pay the ransom.

5. Where was Jemmy able to hide?
 a. up in a tree
 b. the hollow of a dead tree
 c. behind a huge boulder
 d. a passing coach

Name _____

1. Why did Hold-Your-Nose Billy think that Jemmy was actually the Prince?
 a. Jemmy was carrying the crown.
 b. The Prince refused to bow to Jemmy.
 c. Jemmy was able to write.
 d. Billy had seen a poster of Prince Jemmy.

2. What did the outlaws have Jemmy do to prove his letter did not have any hidden messages?
 a. reread the letter from beginning to end
 b. take the letter to the local book reader
 c. ask the Prince to read the letter out loud
 d. reread the letter backwards, word for word

3. What did Prince Brat threaten to do if he was asked to take the message to the King?
 a. find the nearest rock, sit on it, then refuse to move
 b. shout out for the royal guards
 c. tear up the message and keep the crown
 d. tell the King that Jemmy was pretending to be him

4. What animal frightened the boys after they escaped?
 a. a wolf
 b. an alligator
 c. a turtle
 d. a bear

5. How had the appearance of the boys changed?
 a. Their hair was full of dirt.
 b. They were thinner from not eating for days.
 c. Their clothes were torn and dirty.
 d. They were clean after swimming in the lake.

Cooperative Learning & Literature
Kagan Publishing • (800) 933-2667 • www.KaganOnline.com

Recall Questions
The Whipping Boy • Chapters 15–20

❏ **RallyCoach Directions:** Take turns answering each question as your partner coaches. Explain your thinking to your coach.

❏ **Sage-N-Scribe Directions:** The Sage describes what he or she knows about the question so the Scribe can answer the question. The Sage and Scribe switch roles for each question.

Name _____

1. **What was Jemmy's plan for getting food?**
   a. begging for food in the streets
   b. gathering driftwood to sell as firewood
   c. collecting rats for meat
   d. stealing from the hot potato man

2. **Why did Jemmy decide to ride with Captain Nips on the front of the coach?**
   a. He did not want to ride with a bear.
   b. He wanted to protect the Prince from soldiers.
   c. He wanted to watch for road hazards.
   d. He planned to run away at his first chance.

3. **Why did the Prince want to carry the water?**
   a. He did not want to drink water from a servant.
   b. He had never been allowed to carry anything before.
   c. Jemmy refused to carry water for the Prince.
   d. The Prince wanted to help Jemmy for being kind.

4. **What did Jemmy read about himself while in town?**
   a. The Prince had returned to the castle.
   b. Hold-Your-Nose-Billy was captured!
   c. Jemmy was charged with selling the Prince to gypsies.
   d. Jemmy was to return to the castle for a reward.

Name _____

1. **How did Prince Brat react when he was whipped for the first time?**
   a. set his jaws and did not let a sound escape
   b. screamed and yelled
   c. bawled
   d. declared the outlaws would be hung

2. **Why did the King's soldiers not notice the Prince?**
   a. The Prince was dressed in rags.
   b. Jemmy told the soldiers the Prince was gone.
   c. A bear poked his head out of the coach.
   d. The coach smelled of boiled potatoes.

3. **What terrible offense did Smudge commit?**
   a. shaking hands with a prince
   b. whipping a prince
   c. catching rats in the sewer
   d. taking a prince into the sewer

4. **What happened to Cutwater and Hold-Your-Nose-Billy after being captured?**
   a. They were sentenced to live in the sewers.
   b. They were sent to Convict Island.
   c. They were hung and forced to do the jig.
   d. They were placed in the prison towers.

Recall Questions
The Whipping Boy • End-of-Book

Directions: Participate in Find Someone Who to answer the recall questions about *The Whipping Boy*. Write the answer in the space provided. Have your partner initial the answer.

1 What did Jemmy plan to do with the battered birdcage he found?	**2** Why didn't Prince Brat receive his own whippings at the castle?	**3** What did Billy ask Jemmy to do to prove his message did not contain hidden messages?
_____ Initials	_____ Initials	_____ Initials
4 Who gave the boys a ride to town in his coach?	**5** Why did the Prince visit Jemmy's chamber requesting a manservant?	**6** What happened to Hold-Your-Nose-Billy and Cutwater after being caught in the sewers?
_____ Initials	_____ Initials	_____ Initials
7 Why caused Billy to think Jemmy was the Prince?	**8** What law did Smudge, Jemmy's friend, break when he met the Prince?	**9** Who rescued the Prince from his first whipping?
_____ Initials	_____ Initials	_____ Initials

Cooperative Learning & Literature
Kagan Publishing • (800) 933-2667 • www.KaganOnline.com

Journal Writing
The Whipping Boy • Chapter 1

Directions: Think about the Journal Question, and then write your own response. When done, RoundRobin share your writing with your teammates. Use the space at the bottom to record ideas your teammates share.

Journal Question
How does having a whipping boy affect the Prince's behavior? Explain.

Journal Response: _____

_____

_____

_____

_____

_____

_____

_____

_____

_____

_____

_____

Ideas Teammates Shared

Journal Writing
The Whipping Boy • Chapter 9

Directions: Think about the Journal Question, and then write your own response. When done, RoundRobin share your writing with your teammates. Use the space at the bottom to record ideas your teammates share.

Journal Question
Jemmy tricked the outlaws by making them think he was the Prince and told them to send the ransom note with his whipping boy. Will his plan work? Why or why not?

Journal Response: _____

_____

_____

_____

_____

_____

_____

_____

_____

_____

_____

Ideas Teammates Shared

Cooperative Learning & Literature
Kagan Publishing • (800) 933-2667 • www.KaganOnline.com

Journal Writing
The Whipping Boy • Chapter 20

Directions: Think about the Journal Question, and then write your own response. When done, RoundRobin share your writing with your teammates. Use the space at the bottom to record ideas your teammates share.

Journal Question
What lesson can you learn after reading *The Whipping Boy*? Explain.

Journal Response: _____

_____

_____

_____

_____

_____

_____

_____

_____

_____

Ideas Teammates Shared

Journal Writing
The Whipping Boy • End-of-Book

Directions: Think about the Journal Question, and then write your own response. When done, RoundRobin share your writing with your teammates. Use the space at the bottom to record ideas your teammates share.

Journal Question

How would have Jemmy's life been different if he remained in the sewers rather than becoming the official whipping boy? Use story details to support your answer.

Journal Response: _____

_____

_____

_____

_____

_____

_____

_____

_____

_____

_____

Ideas Teammates Shared

Cooperative Learning & Literature
Kagan Publishing • (800) 933-2667 • www.KaganOnline.com

Higher-Level Thinking Cards
The Whipping Boy

Directions: Copy enough cards so that each student receives a Question Card. Have students stand up, pair up, and do Traveling Pair Share to respond to each other's questions. Students trade cards and find a new partner to share.

---

① The Whipping Boy

What advantages did Jemmy have being the official whipping boy?

Traveling Pair Share

---

② The Whipping Boy

What did the Prince learn during his time with Jemmy?

Traveling Pair Share

---

③ The Whipping Boy

How did the Prince change from the beginning to the end of the story?

Traveling Pair Share

---

④ The Whipping Boy

Evaluate and explain Prince Horace's reaction to learning his nickname was Prince Brat.

Traveling Pair Share

---

⑤ The Whipping Boy

Several laws exist regarding how to treat the Prince. How do these laws affect Prince Horace? Evaluate and explain.

Traveling Pair Share

---

⑥ The Whipping Boy

The story of the whipping boy is a work of imagination but it is true that in the past some royal households had whipping boys. What do you think about this fact?

Traveling Pair Share

---

⑦ The Whipping Boy

Was it right of Jemmy to allow the Prince to shake Smudge's hand and carry water? Why?

Traveling Pair Share

---

⑧ The Whipping Boy

Compare and contrast Jemmy's life in the sewers to his life as a whipping boy. What were the benefits and disadvantages of both?

Traveling Pair Share

Higher-Level Thinking Cards
The Whipping Boy

Directions: Copy enough cards so that each student receives a Question Card. Have students stand up, pair up, and do Traveling Pair Share to respond to each other's questions. Students trade cards and find a new partner to share.

⑨ The Whipping Boy

What do you think caused Prince Horace to change his opinion about Jemmy? Explain.

Traveling Pair Share

⑩ The Whipping Boy

How would you persuade the King to not have a whipping boy? Explain.

Traveling Pair Share

⑪ The Whipping Boy

How does Prince Brat betray Jemmy during their capture? What does this say about his character?

Traveling Pair Share

⑫ The Whipping Boy

What was difficult about being a prince during this time period? Explain.

Traveling Pair Share

⑬ The Whipping Boy

Whose life was better, Jemmy's or Prince Horace's? Explain.

Traveling Pair Share

⑭ The Whipping Boy

What do you think will happen to Jemmy after the story ends?

Traveling Pair Share

⑮ The Whipping Boy

Why do you think Jemmy wanted to return to his old life in the streets? Explain.

Traveling Pair Share

⑯ The Whipping Boy

Why do you think Prince Brat did not make a sound when he was whipped? What did he learn from Jemmy?

Traveling Pair Share

Cooperative Learning & Literature
Kagan Publishing • (800) 933-2667 • www.KaganOnline.com

Activities for Any Literature Selection

Sequencing

☐ **RallyCoach Directions:** Take turns sequencing the main events from the story. Discuss your thinking with your coach and make sure your coach agrees before writing.

☐ **Sage-N-Scribe Directions:** The Sage instructs the Scribe what event to add next to the sequence. The Sage and Scribe switch roles to add each event.

Book Title: _____

Partner A: _____ Partner B: _____

Partner A:

Next

Partner B:

Next

Partner A:

Next

Partner B:

Next

Partner A:

Next

Partner B:

Higher-Level Thinking Question Cards
Questions for Any Book

Directions: Copy enough cards so that each student receives a Question Card. Have students stand up, pair up, and do Traveling Pair Share to respond to each other's questions. Students trade cards and find a new partner to share.

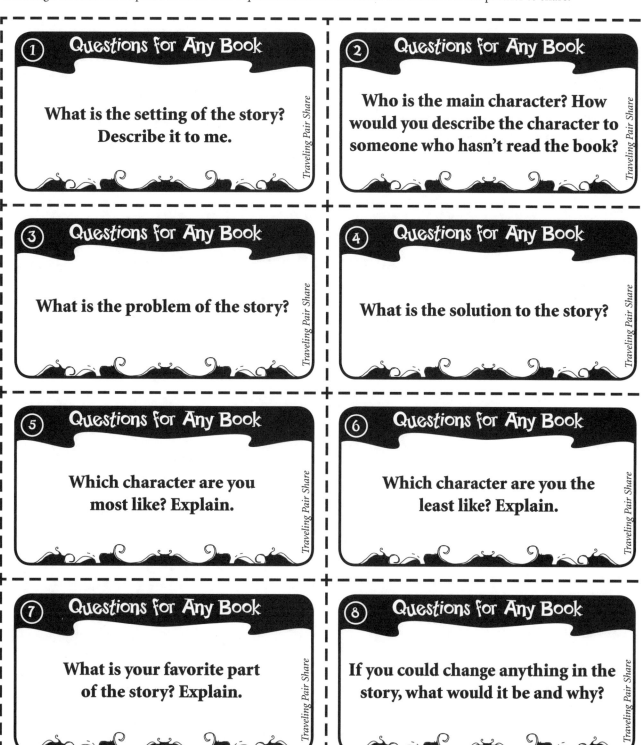

① Questions for Any Book

What is the setting of the story? Describe it to me.

Traveling Pair Share

② Questions for Any Book

Who is the main character? How would you describe the character to someone who hasn't read the book?

Traveling Pair Share

③ Questions for Any Book

What is the problem of the story?

Traveling Pair Share

④ Questions for Any Book

What is the solution to the story?

Traveling Pair Share

⑤ Questions for Any Book

Which character are you most like? Explain.

Traveling Pair Share

⑥ Questions for Any Book

Which character are you the least like? Explain.

Traveling Pair Share

⑦ Questions for Any Book

What is your favorite part of the story? Explain.

Traveling Pair Share

⑧ Questions for Any Book

If you could change anything in the story, what would it be and why?

Traveling Pair Share

Higher-Level Thinking Question Cards
Questions for Any Book

Directions: Copy enough cards so that each student receives a Question Card. Have students stand up, pair up, and do Traveling Pair Share to respond to each other's questions. Students trade cards and find a new partner to share.

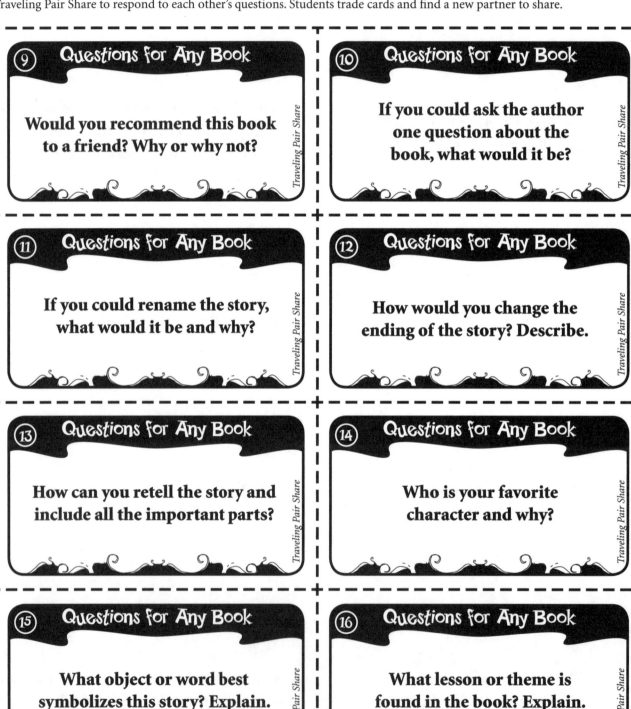

⑨ Questions for Any Book

Would you recommend this book to a friend? Why or why not?

Traveling Pair Share

⑩ Questions for Any Book

If you could ask the author one question about the book, what would it be?

Traveling Pair Share

⑪ Questions for Any Book

If you could rename the story, what would it be and why?

Traveling Pair Share

⑫ Questions for Any Book

How would you change the ending of the story? Describe.

Traveling Pair Share

⑬ Questions for Any Book

How can you retell the story and include all the important parts?

Traveling Pair Share

⑭ Questions for Any Book

Who is your favorite character and why?

Traveling Pair Share

⑮ Questions for Any Book

What object or word best symbolizes this story? Explain.

Traveling Pair Share

⑯ Questions for Any Book

What lesson or theme is found in the book? Explain.

Traveling Pair Share

Cooperative Learning & Literature
Kagan Publishing • (800) 933-2667 • www.KaganOnline.com

Higher-Level Thinking Question Cards
Questions for Any Book

Directions: Copy enough cards so that each student receives a Question Card. Have students stand up, pair up, and do Traveling Pair Share to respond to each other's questions. Students trade cards and find a new partner to share.

17 Questions for Any Book
What feelings did you experience as you read this book? For example, were you sad, happy, angry, or confused?

18 Questions for Any Book
If you wanted to learn more about the author or something from the book, how would you locate the information?

19 Questions for Any Book
Have you read another book that is similar to this story? Describe the similarities.

20 Questions for Any Book
What will happen after the book or story ends?

21 Questions for Any Book
How would you persuade someone to read the story?

22 Questions for Any Book
Can you connect any part of this story to your life? Describe.

23 Questions for Any Book
What was your favorite passage in the book? Explain why.

24 Questions for Any Book
Do you have a friend who has similar character traits as someone in the story? Describe.

Higher-Level Thinking Question Cards
Comparing a Book to Its Movie

Directions: Copy enough cards so that each student receives a Question Card. Have students stand up, pair up, and do Traveling Pair Share to respond to each other's questions. Students trade cards and find a new partner to share.

① **Comparing a Book to Its Movie**

In your opinion, what was better, the book or the movie? Why?

Traveling Pair Share

② **Comparing a Book to Its Movie**

Was there anything that happened in the movie that wasn't in the book?

Traveling Pair Share

③ **Comparing a Book to Its Movie**

Was there anything that happened in the book that wasn't in the movie?

Traveling Pair Share

④ **Comparing a Book to Its Movie**

What was your favorite part of the movie? Was this part better than the book? Explain.

Traveling Pair Share

⑤ **Comparing a Book to Its Movie**

What was your favorite part of the book? Was this part better than the movie? Explain.

Traveling Pair Share

⑥ **Comparing a Book to Its Movie**

If you could change something about the movie, what would it be and why?

Traveling Pair Share

⑦ **Comparing a Book to Its Movie**

Would you recommend this movie to other people who have read the book? Why or why not?

Traveling Pair Share

⑧ **Comparing a Book to Its Movie**

How would you make the movie more like the book? Explain.

Traveling Pair Share

Cooperative Learning & Literature
Kagan Publishing • (800) 933-2667 • www.KaganOnline.com

Higher-Level Thinking Question Cards
Comparing a Book to Its Movie

Directions: Copy enough cards so that each student receives a Question Card. Have students stand up, pair up, and do Traveling Pair Share to respond to each other's questions. Students trade cards and find a new partner to share.

⑨ Comparing a Book to Its Movie

Were you disappointed in the movie? Why or why not?

Traveling Pair Share

⑩ Comparing a Book to Its Movie

Was the movie what you had visualized as you read the book? Explain.

Traveling Pair Share

⑪ Comparing a Book to Its Movie

Did the movie story differ from the story that was told in the book? Explain.

Traveling Pair Share

⑫ Comparing a Book to Its Movie

Imagine you were the director of the movie. What would be one thing you would NOT change that happened in the book? Why?

Traveling Pair Share

⑬ Comparing a Book to Its Movie

Do you think it is positive or negative to have the movie differ from the book? Explain.

Traveling Pair Share

⑭ Comparing a Book to Its Movie

Was there one character in the movie who was exactly like you visualized from the book? Explain.

Traveling Pair Share

⑮ Comparing a Book to Its Movie

Would you recommend reading the book before seeing the movie? Why?

Traveling Pair Share

⑯ Comparing a Book to Its Movie

Would you recommend seeing the movie before reading the book? Why?

Traveling Pair Share

Journal Writing

Directions: Think about the Journal Question, and then write your own response. When done, RoundRobin share your writing with your teammates. Use the space at the bottom to record ideas your teammates share.

Journal Question

Journal Response: _____

_____

_____

_____

_____

_____

_____

_____

_____

_____

_____

_____

_____

Ideas Teammates Shared

Cooperative Learning & Literature
Kagan Publishing • (800) 933-2667 • www.KaganOnline.com

Journal Writing
Before Reading Guide

Directions: Before you read (either a book or chapter), independently fill out the "Me" section of the form. Then, do a RoundRobin. Fill out the "My Teammates" section using ideas your teammates share.

Name _____

Me	My Teammates
I predict: _____ _____ _____ _____	My teammates predict: _____ _____ _____ _____
I wonder: _____ _____ _____ _____	My teammates wonder: _____ _____ _____ _____
I imagine: _____ _____ _____ _____	My teammates imagine: _____ _____ _____ _____
I think: _____ _____ _____ _____	My teammates think: _____ _____ _____ _____

Journal Writing
After Reading Guide

Directions: After you read (either a book or chapter) discuss each reading strategy aloud with your group. Record what your teammates says. Students may write individual answers first, then discuss while recording teammates' answers.

Name _____

Me	My Teammates
I predict: _____ _____ _____ _____	My teammates predict: _____ _____ _____ _____
I wonder: _____ _____ _____ _____	My teammates wonder: _____ _____ _____ _____
I imagine: _____ _____ _____ _____	My teammates imagine: _____ _____ _____ _____
I think: _____ _____ _____ _____	My teammates think: _____ _____ _____ _____

Cooperative Learning & Literature
Kagan Publishing • (800) 933-2667 • www.KaganOnline.com

Recall Questions
Book Review

Directions: Participate in Find Someone Who to answer the recall questions about the book. Write the answer in the space provided. Have your partner initial the answer.

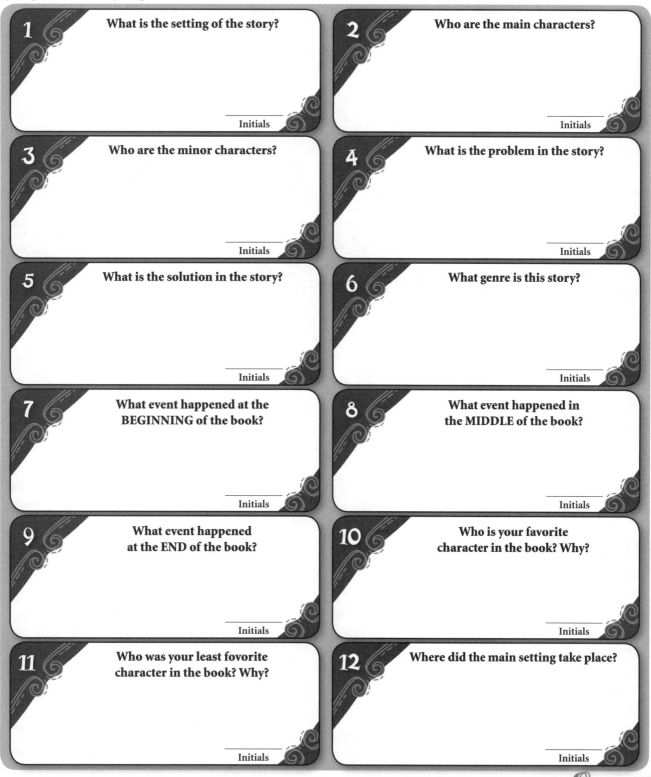

1 What is the setting of the story?

_____ Initials

2 Who are the main characters?

_____ Initials

3 Who are the minor characters?

_____ Initials

4 What is the problem in the story?

_____ Initials

5 What is the solution in the story?

_____ Initials

6 What genre is this story?

_____ Initials

7 What event happened at the BEGINNING of the book?

_____ Initials

8 What event happened in the MIDDLE of the book?

_____ Initials

9 What event happened at the END of the book?

_____ Initials

10 Who is your favorite character in the book? Why?

_____ Initials

11 Who was your least favorite character in the book? Why?

_____ Initials

12 Where did the main setting take place?

_____ Initials

Recall Questions
Chapter Review

Directions: Participate in Find Someone Who to answer the recall questions about the book. Write the answer in the space provided. Have your partner initial the answer.

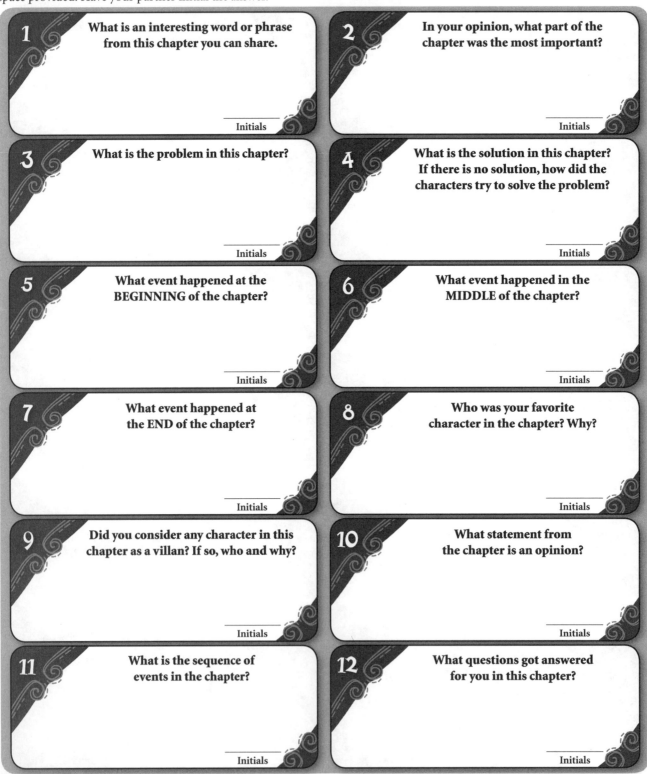

1 What is an interesting word or phrase from this chapter you can share.

Initials

2 In your opinion, what part of the chapter was the most important?

Initials

3 What is the problem in this chapter?

Initials

4 What is the solution in this chapter? If there is no solution, how did the characters try to solve the problem?

Initials

5 What event happened at the BEGINNING of the chapter?

Initials

6 What event happened in the MIDDLE of the chapter?

Initials

7 What event happened at the END of the chapter?

Initials

8 Who was your favorite character in the chapter? Why?

Initials

9 Did you consider any character in this chapter as a villan? If so, who and why?

Initials

10 What statement from the chapter is an opinion?

Initials

11 What is the sequence of events in the chapter?

Initials

12 What questions got answered for you in this chapter?

Initials

Cooperative Learning & Literature
Kagan Publishing • (800) 933-2667 • www.KaganOnline.com

Literature Answer Key

Amber Brown Is Not a Crayon

✦ RallyCoach/Sage-N-Scribe (pp. 35–37)

Page 35

Left Side
1) c. 3rd grade
2) b. flicks the lights off
3) d. They are able to finish each other's sentences.
4) a. Soon you will be going on a new journey and beginning a new life.
5) c. She told her alligators are in the toilet.

Right Side
1) a. messy
2) d. China
3) c. His dad got a new job.
4) b. Oreo® cookies
5) a. baseball player

Page 36

Left Side
1) d. *Charlotte's Web*
2) c. a "Sold" sticker on the For Sale sign
3) a. peanut butter and M&M's® sandwich
4) c. give him part of Amber's allowance
5) b. fractions

Right Side
1) b. He was being a kangaroo.
2) b. He flew to see Mr. Daniels and to look for a new house.
3) b. France
4) d. Amber can store some of her stuff in Justin's desk.
5) c. His new school has a cafeteria.

Page 37

Left Side
1) c. a natural disaster
2) c. Hannah is too neat and wants to look good.
3) b. chicken pox
4) a. *"Finally!"*

Right Side
1) d. He threw away their chewing gum ball.
2) a. double-fudge brownie mix, unbaked
3) c. had a pizza party
4) b. the chewing gum ball

✦ Fan-N-Pick/Showdown (pp. 38–39)

Page 38
1) made monkey sounds
2) He wouldn't talk about leaving.
3) had a pizza party
4) China
5) There were alligators in the toilet.
6) He got a new job.
7) chewing gum ball
8) 3rd grade

Page 39
9) Justin was good at pasting and Amber had better handwriting.
10) an Alabama sweat shirt
11) Passport
12) She does not want to have to pass out little packets of peanuts.
13) the picture on her passport
14) a rake
15) Danny-the-Bratster
16) chopsticks

~Literature Answer Key~

Because of Winn-Dixie

✦ Find Someone Who (pp. 51–56)

Page 51
1) a. summer
4) c. The store's name was Winn-Dixie.
7) c. Preacher got a job at the Naomi church.

2) b. The dog smiled.
5) c. Opal
8) c. He was always preaching or thinking about preaching.

3) c. Opal told the manager it was her dog.
6) c. shaggy rug with bald spots
9) d. laid his head in Preacher's lap

Page 52
1) b. bathed him
4) b. a turtle
7) b. An entire library full of books

2) c. He kept sneezing.
5) b. pulled the toilet paper off the roll
8) c. threw a book at him

3) b. being a preacher's wife
6) d. A mouse ran across the floor.
9) d. realistic fiction

Page 53
1) b. A sign was posted that read: NO DOGS ALLOWED.
4) c. invited Opal to her birthday party
7) c. her heart

2) c. offering to sweep, dust, and take out the trash at the store
5) a. a dog-eating witch
8) b. good gardener

3) b. The bird squawked, *"DOG!"*
6) b. She dislikes it because other students called her "lunch meat."
9) c. wait-and-see tree

Page 54
1) b. thunderstorms
4) b. He would break away from her bike and run.
7) a. *Gone with the Wind*

2) d. Otis was playing his guitar for the animals.
5) c. She should try to be their friends.
8) b. 14

3) c. Otis knew what it was like to be locked up.
6) b. There were bottles hanging from the branches.
9) c. His family had died and his house was burned down.

Page 55
1) a. build a candy factory
4) c. Her brother drowned the year before.
7) c. dogs

2) b. It made the eaters feel sad.
5) b. He sang his songs on the street and refused to stop.
8) a. It would be cooler.

3) c. She wanted to keep her ghosts away.
6) a. She would invite the Dewberry boys.
9) a. pickles

Page 56
1) b. Winn-Dixie couldn't be found.
4) b. Everyone was singing.
7) a. She didn't know any songs.

2) c. He has a pathological fear of thunderstorms.
5) c. under Gloria's bed
8) b. You can't hold onto something that wants to go, only love it while you have it.

3) d. Opal
6) c. He offered his hand to help her up.
9) c. to entertain the reader about a girl who makes unlikely friends

～Literature Answer Key～

Because of Winn-Dixie continued

✦ Fan-N-Pick/Showdown (pp. 57–58)

Page 57
1) plant a tree
2) under Gloria Dump's bed
3) put his head in Preacher's lap
4) She loved Opal very much.
5) play music in the streets
6) the store where he was found
7) thunderstorms
8) invited Opal to her birthday party

Page 58
9) *Gone with the Wind*
10) Her dad built the library for her birthday.
11) Her brother Carson died the year before.
12) Littmus Lozenge
13) She could not cook.
14) He sneezed.
15) They thought she was a witch.
16) produce section

The Boxcar Children

✦ RallyCoach/Sage-N-Scribe (pp. 67–72)

Page 67

Left Side
1) b. the past
2) c. She did not like Benny and he would be a lot of work.
3) c. They do not want to be seen by others.
4) d. a piece of bread and water
5) c. a drinking fountain

Right Side
1) c. a red bench at the bakery
2) a. The grandfather did not like their mother.
3) a. bear
4) b. The baker was going to Greenfield.
5) d. They were fast asleep.

Page 68

Left Side
1) b. an old boxcar in the woods
2) b. Jessie
3) d. a brook near the boxcar
4) a. a dog walking with a sore paw
5) b. The dog is very gentle and kind.

Right Side
1) c. a tree stump
2) c. He was afraid the engine would come back.
3) b. blueberries
4) b. Jessie
5) a. a tin cup

Page 69

Left Side
1) b. a spot behind a small waterfall
2) d. a cracked pink cup
3) b. a bone
4) c. bag of cookies
5) d. He heard a stick crack in the woods.

Right Side
1) c. a dump
2) d. She rinsed them with boiling water.
3) a. mowing a lawn
4) b. yellow sweet butter
5) b. Watch was no longer worried.

Page 70

Left Side
1) b. thinning out the vegetable garden
2) b. a fireplace
3) d. bent nails
4) c. washed the stockings
5) b. hen eggs

Right Side
1) d. She was curious about Henry.
2) c. He likes to get things in order.
3) b. a swimming pool
4) d. The children had worked really hard.
5) a. a black kettle

~ Literature Answer Key ~

The Boxcar Children

✦ RallyCoach/Sage-N-Scribe (pp. 67–72) continued

Page 71

Left Side
1) b. Grandfather seeing them
2) d. The children were so happy while working.
3) a. Field Day
4) b. He did not want anyone to know his last name.
5) c. He would not let Watch be a better reader.

Right Side
1) d. carrying and filling little baskets
2) c. a newspaper
3) c. Henry's grandfather gave out the prize money.
4) c. gave it to Jessie
5) a. using a fire under the hot stones

Page 72

Left Side
1) b. a bear out of stockings
2) c. Violet could not stop crying.
3) a. Violet was very sick.
4) c. Benny would have to go to school.
5) d. Ask the lady if she would be willing to take another dog.

Right Side
1) a. cut a J on one side
2) b. They would have to tell them their names.
3) b. Dr. Moore followed Henry home one night.
4) b. the floor next to Jessie's bed
5) b. Watch was being waited on by a maid.

Frindle

✦ RallyCoach/Sage-N-Scribe (pp. 87–91)

Page 87

Left Side
1) c. turned his classroom into a tropical island.
2) a. language arts
3) d. use the dictionary
4) c. strict
5) a. homework first

Right Side
1) d. Nick was screeching the word, "*peep.*"
2) b. x-ray vision
3) a. pleased to have a teacher take her work seriously
4) c. assigned Nick a report
5) c. encyclopedia sets

Page 88

Left Side
1) c. waste as much time as possible
2) a. Nick wanted to listen to his music.
3) a. ask for frindles at the Penny Pantry
4) b. annoyed about the inappropriate use of a word
5) b. to prove when the letter was written and then never opened

Right Side
1) a. treated him like a teacher's pet
2) b. a word Nick made up to mean pen
3) b. asked Nick to stay after class
4) d. realistic fiction
5) c. The principal went to talk with Mr. and Mrs. Allen.

Page 89

Left Side
1) c. Mrs. Chatham
2) d. It is an overreaction to an experiment with language.
3) b. a writer for *The Westfield Gazette*
4) c. war of the words

Right Side
1) a. the lack of respect for authority
2) b. The word ain't is found in the dictionary.
3) b. America is a free country with a free press.
4) d. "*What is the meaning of this?*"

Cooperative Learning & Literature
Kagan Publishing • (800) 933-2667 • www.KaganOnline.com

~Literature Answer Key~

Frindle continued

✦ RallyCoach/Sage-N-Scribe (pp. 87–91) continued

Page 90

Left Side
1) b. He was shy and awkward.
2) a. to watch what he said so he didn't offend anyone
3) c. All words in the dictionary were made by people, so Nick wanted to see if it were true, and fun to do.
4) b. Bud owed Nick the money from the first 3 weeks' profit.

Right Side
1) a. pleased that Nick invented a brand-new word
2) c. Both words were invented for no particular reason.
3) a. Bud wanted to use the word frindle to sell and would give Nick 30 percent of profits.
4) b. All the merchandise with frindle was selling quickly.

Page 91

Left Side
1) b. She enjoyed having him as a student and expects great things from him in the future.
2) c. It contained the word frindle.
3) a. She had actually helped the word become popular.
4) b. A gold fountain pen with an inscription from Nick

Right Side
1) d. The frindle trust fund from frindle was legally Nick's.
2) d. She was purposely the villain for Nick's story.
3) b. It was Nick because he wanted a way to thank her.
4) b. 45 years

✦ Find Someone Who (p. 92)

1) 5th grade language arts teacher
2) a dictionary
3) for using the word frindle in class
4) held up pens or frindles
5) She really wanted the word to be a success.
6) assigned Nick a report on the origin of words
7) make it a trademark and use it on pens, shirts, etc.
8) a reporter for the *Westfield Gazette*
9) a gold fountain pen
10) made "peep" noises
11) pen
12) It contained the word frindle.

Gooney Bird Greene

✦ RallyCoach/Sage-N-Scribe (pp. 103–105)

Page 103

Left Side
1) b. October
2) d. her own dictionary
3) a. characters
4) d. She wanted to be the center of attention.
5) c. absolutely true stories

Right Side
1) c. China
2) b. He stuck an origami star up his nose.
3) c. Gooney Bird Greene
4) b. her name
5) d. flying carpet

Page 104

Left Side
1) c. correcting spelling papers
2) a. rolled up carpet from the front porch
3) b. 2nd grade
4) c. large black poodle
5) d. a gumball machine

Right Side
1) b. Her dad got a new job in Watertower.
2) c. The car ran over a pot hole.
3) c. They screw into her ears.
4) a. Gooney began describing the clothing and didn't have enough suspense.
5) c. an ice cream shop

~Literature Answer Key~

Gooney Bird Greene continued

✦ RallyCoach/Sage-N-Scribe (pp. 103–105)

Page 105

Left Side
1) c. Gooney Birde was not in class.
2) a. suddenly
3) c. The orchestra came to play a saraband.
4) a. Mrs. Pidgeon interrupted.
5) a. He was a special dentist who makes teeth.

Right Side
1) b. She had to direct an orchestra.
2) d. Everyone could see her pointing her finger.
3) a. takes a deep breath
4) b. The cat was in love with the cow.
5) c. invisible

✦ Find Someone Who (p. 106)

1) He was consumed or in love with the cow.
2) a beginning, middle, and end
3) Town Hall Auditorium
4) China
5) Forty-three pairs of teeth
6) 2nd grade
7) true
8) He put origami stars up his nose.
9) a gumball machine
10) She flew out of her car on a carpet.
11) gumballs
12) a gooney bird

Gregor the Overlander

✦ Find Someone Who (pp. 117–122)

Page 117
1) a. six
2) c. to always stay in the present and not look into the future
3) c. a queen or princess
4) a. Bats encircled them.
5) b. The water must lead out of the palace.
6) d. Gregor had to watch Boots.
7) b. poked her in the eye
8) c. the largest cockroach he has ever seen
9) c. fantasy

Page 118
1) c. a keychain he made at camp
2) b. He saw the face of a monstrous rat.
3) d. Luxa
4) a. fight or be killed
5) b. no eyes
6) a. around 3,000
7) b. stabbed and thrown into the river
8) c. He would need it once he got out of Regalia.
9) c. Eat them.

Page 119
1) b. It was his father's favorite drink and reminded him of home.
2) a. Gregor was bruising him by holding on too tight.
3) c. She really liked them.
4) a. Luxa
5) c. two
6) b. spider
7) a. built a wall blocking the tunnel
8) d. light
9) c. rats

Cooperative Learning & Literature
Kagan Publishing • (800) 933-2667 • www.KaganOnline.com

∽Literature Answer Key∾

Gregor the Overlander continued

✦ Find Someone Who (pp. 117–122) continued

Page 120

1) a. eight
4) b. diapers
7) a. all humans were dead

2) a. Ripred, the rat
5) d. make sandwiches
8) b. A spider spun a web around their legs.

3) c. The cockroaches
6) b. a can of root beer
9) b. Vikus sent them to join the quest.

Page 121

1) b. Henry
4) b. broke his bond for life by letting Henry fall and saving Gregor instead
7) c. when Tick died to save his sister

2) c. sewed up her wing
5) b. to keep their teeth at a manageable length
8) c. a compass

3) d. Tick
6) a. His dad was wearing a coat of rat fur.
9) b. Henry

Page 122

1) c. They needed to wash off the smell of the Overland for their protection.
4) b. in a dripping tunnel
7) b. She could tell the difference between the cockroaches
10) d. Gregor

2) b. the Prophecy of Gray
5) a. Henry
8) a. Vikus
11) d. Ripred

3) c. by the bridge
6) d. four
9) b. a cockroach
12) a. Boots

Henry and Ribsy

✦ RallyCoach/Sage-N-Scribe (pp. 133–139)

Page 133

Left Side

1) b. chasing the Grumbies' cat
2) d. ate a police officer's sandwich
3) b. keep Ribsy out of trouble for 1 month

Right Side

1) c. "*Can I ride up on the grease rack?*"
2) a. He wanted some milk to go with his lunch.
3) d. Woofies

Page 134

Left Side

1) b. 15 cents extra a week in his allowance
2) a. biting someone
3) b. Ramona was pulling at Ribsy's tail
4) d. Scooter took Henry's bike out of the garage.

Right Side

1) c. growled deep at the garbage man
2) a. The garbage smelled bad.
3) b. He was being a protective watchdog.
4) b. Mrs. Huggins would take out the garbage if Henry clipped around the edge of the lawn.

Page 135

Left Side

1) c. electric clippers
2) d. wear a sailor's hat
3) c. eating a pound of butter

Right Side

1) a. embarrassed by the chewed up look of the haircut
2) a. brainstorm ways to pull his teeth
3) b. It was past the Fourth of July.

~Literature Answer Key~

Henry and Ribsy continued

✦ RallyCoach/Sage-N-Scribe (pp. 133–139) continued

Page 136
Left Side
1) b. He kept wiggling his teeth with his tongue.
2) c. They were making fun of him.
3) a. tied a string to his teeth and had Ribsy pull on the rope attached to the string

Right Side
1) a. The cost of living has gone up.
2) b. They got bad hair cuts as well.
3) b. spit double

Page 137
Left Side
1) a. She was at the PTA meeting.
2) b. She was pretending it was a camera.
3) a. She took his bone.
4) b. Ramona was terrified of Ribsy.

Right Side
1) c. Beezus invited Henry to play checkers.
2) c. ate Ramona's ice cream
3) c. She thought Henry and Beezus were spelling something she couldn't have.
4) c. Miss Mullen told her to get down.

Page 138
Left Side
1) c. He was looking for his tin pants.
2) a. Mr. Grumbie
3) b. chilly and rainy
4) a. Another fisherman fished him out of the water.

Right Side
1) c. Mom said she was on vacation
2) c. drop his line overboard and let it be carried out
3) a. He jumped over the side of the boat.
4) c. His chance to catch a salmon was gone.

Page 139
Left Side
1) a. People were making comments about a smelly dog.
2) b. a salmon
3) a. He wanted everyone to know it was his fish.
4) b. confused that Henry caught a fish bare-handed

Right Side
1) c. Scooter fishing with his dad
2) d. He tackled the fish with his bare hands.
3) c. 29 pounds
4) d. Ribsy found the salmon Henry caught.

✦ Find Someone Who (p. 140)

1) Ribsy growled at the man.
2) Ribsy
3) Chinook salmon
4) tackled one in shallow water
5) ride up in the service rack
6) Ribsy
7) wear a sailor's hat
8) He jumped out of the boat.
9) keep Ribsy out of trouble
10) She took his bone.
11) He wanted to be a watchdog.
12) electric clippers

Cooperative Learning & Literature
Kagan Publishing • (800) 933-2667 • www.KaganOnline.com

～Literature Answer Key～

Little House in the Big Woods

✦ RallyCoach/Sage-N-Scribe (pp. 159–164)

Page 159
Left Side
1) c. the woods of Wisconsin
2) d. to eat in the winter months
3) b. to demonstrate the hard work it takes to get food
4) d. The weather was getting colder.
5) b. baking and churning

Right Side
1) a. The wolves would eat little girls.
2) a. He prevented the pig from being eaten.
3) c. as a ball to be kicked and bounced
4) b. It was so cold, the meat was frozen in the shed.
5) c. kerosene lamp

Page 160
Left Side
1) a. to show how important the gun is to Pa
2) d. A wounded animal could kill a man before reloading his gun.
3) d. a screech-owl in the trees
4) b. a bracket for her China woman
5) d. rag doll

Right Side
1) c. On hooks above the door
2) b. He dare not return without the cows.
3) b. Obey your parents.
4) c. A panther was roaming near in the woods.
5) b. hot baked potatoes

Page 161
Left Side
1) c. She must sit quietly and listen to stories.
2) a. Their father kept them busy working, and they had chores.
3) b. It is easier to be good now than when Grandpa was a boy.
4) d. carrying the lantern
5) b. pretty calico fabric

Right Side
1) c. Pa told her a story about Grandpa's sled.
2) c. They ran into and picked up a hog.
3) a. It was her birthday.
4) a. a black bear
5) c. It was hard to see, and he thought a tree stump was a bear.

Page 162
Left Side
1) b. to help the reader understand the old objects
2) d. a snow that means men can make more sugar
3) a. The family got up to leave before the sun.
4) c. It was a special soap to use for special times.
5) a. Grandma

Right Side
1) a. the blood of the tree
2) b. She got to wear her delaine dress.
3) c. He was once in war.
4) d. in awe of the beautiful dresses and fun dances
5) c. to eat Grandma's new syrup

Page 163
Left Side
1) c. Laura's feet were soft from wearing shoes.
2) c. 7 miles
3) c. The town houses were made of boards.
4) b. the weight of the rocks she collected
5) a. gathering eggs

Right Side
1) b. baby deer
2) a. small and frightened
3) d. calico fabric for a new apron
4) c. Laura liked to run and climb trees too.
5) c. The bees could not get into the thick fur.

~ Literature Answer Key ~

Little House in the Big Woods continued

✦ RallyCoach/Sage-N-Scribe (pp. 159–164) continued

Page 164

Left Side
1) b. The crops would all be lost.
2) c. brought the men fresh water
3) d. mud plaster and a rolled-up sheet
4) b. 2 or 3 days
5) c. sacks of wheat

Right Side
1) a. Charley was not already working in the fields.
2) c. Charley had played tricks on the men earlier.
3) b. It is beginning to become fall.
4) a. It took eight horses to work the machine.
5) c. He was busy loving the beauty of the animals.

✦ Fan-N-Pick/Showdown (pp. 165–166)

Page 165
1) frying the pig's tale and using the pigs bladder like a balloon
2) a screech-owl
3) Prince, the dog
4) They went sledding.
5) to save for company
6) the dance at Grandpa's
7) a stump
8) They were going to town.

Page 166
9) The rocks ripped a hole in her pocket.
10) He had already pretended to be in trouble and was just joking.
11) Mary had pretty golden blond curls.
12) a bear
13) corn meal
14) blood
15) They have never seen a town before.
16) be loud, make noise, run, shout

Ramona Quimby, Age 8

✦ RallyCoach/Sage-N-Scribe (pp. 183–186)

Page 183

Left Side
1) a. getting carsick
2) c. a pearly pink eraser
3) d. Danny
4) c. Ramona's favorite time of day is reading.
5) a. dog

Right Side
1) c. the check-out counter at Shop-Rite Market
2) b. Mrs. Kemp's house
3) b. Superfoot
4) d. Drop Everything and Read
5) c. Ramona said she needed to do her Sustained Silent Reading.

Page 184

Left Side
1) d. a hard-boiled egg
2) c. so the students could see the larvae
3) a. Mrs. Whaley calling Ramona a show-off.
4) c. tongue
5) b. She did not want her parents to think they were hungry.

Right Side
1) a. a popular thing to do
2) c. She is embarrassed about the egg in her hair.
3) c. drawing a picture of his foot
4) a. They have to cook dinner on the weekend.
5) d. try to be extra good

Cooperative Learning & Literature
Kagan Publishing • (800) 933-2667 • www.KaganOnline.com

~Literature Answer Key~

Ramona Quimby, Age 8 continued

✦ RallyCoach/Sage-N-Scribe (pp. 183–186)

Page 185

Left Side
1) d. bring the newspaper in to their dad
2) c. cili powder
3) c. It will take a while to get the kitchen clean.
4) b. Ramona threw up on the floor.
5) c. a taxi

Right Side
1) a. The girls resolved to be extra good on Sunday.
2) c. cream of wheat
3) d. The car could not go into reverse.
4) a. Mrs. Quimby
5) a. It is probably a soda.

Page 186

Left Side
1) b. a cartoon drawn by her father
2) a. Ramona is noisy.
3) b. Make it into a commercial.
4) a. The weather was dreary and rainy.
5) b. going out to dinner

Right Side
1) d. bored and cranky
2) b. some letters and a book
3) c. Ramona kept giggling and forgot her words.
4) d. Ramona has a very messy room.
5) c. The Quimby's looked like a nice family.

✦ Find Someone Who (p. 187)

1) b. He wants to be an art teacher.
3) c. It was the latest fad for 3rd graders.
5) b. Superfoot
7) b. Mrs. Whaley called Ramona a show-off and nuisance.
9) c. The girls complained about the tongue.
11) a. She threw up on the floor.

2) b. The family looked nice.
4) c. out for dinner
6) c. Mrs. Quimby
8) b. a shiny, pink eraser
10) b. Drop Everything and Read
12) c. Mrs. Kemp's house

The Ravenmaster's Secret: Escape from the Tower of London

✦ Find Someone Who (pp. 197–204)

Page 197
1) a. Yeoman Warders
4) d. chamber pots being emptied into the river
7) c. All gates would soon be locked.

2) b. The Tower would fall to the enemies.
5) a. hanging day
8) b. his character

3) c. 1735
6) c. He threw up when he saw the hanging.
9) d. historical fiction

Page 198
1) c. preparing the ravens' meals
4) b. Simon Frick
7) c. to stop those trying to escape

2) a. Tuck
5) c. treason
8) b. a haunting song

3) c. The climbing boys die at a young age.
6) b. the world beyond the Tower walls
9) c. a ginger biscuit from Forrest

Page 199
1) c. toothache
4) d. They were least able to take care of themselves.
7) c. Her nurse, Flora, taught her.

2) b. a good-luck nail
5) b. A large river rat came into her cell.
8) a. He asked where she had been staying the past few weeks.

3) c. What news of my father?
6) b. Ned
9) a. encyclopedia

~Literature Answer Key~

The Ravenmaster's Secret: Escape from the Tower of London *continued*

✦ Find Someone Who (pp. 197–204) *continued*

Page 200
1) b. He only had one pair of shoes.
4) d. A priest gave it to her during his visit.
7) d. trying to put out the fire set to her family home

2) c. Forrest recognized Ned's blue cap.
5) a. to ward off evil
8) c. her ruby ring

3) c. Master Meeks sold Ned in a card game.
6) b. face up to your destiny
9) b. noble blood

Page 201
1) c. showed the new warder Tuck's tricks
4) a. He believed she was innocent.
7) b. a carpenter

2) a. It is wash day.
5) c. jumped into the river and tried to swim away
8) c. Maddy's trial had been denied and she's been sentenced to die by the axe.

3) c. a hole in his pocket
6) c. Ned had burnt his knees and his skin was too delicate.
9) b. bring Maddy her supper

Page 202
1) a. Ned
4) c. Ned needed to catch a rat.
7) c. in an empty barrel

2) b. He was afraid he might never see them again.
5) a. trim her nails
8) b. said *"King George"*

3) b. Ned knew his life wasn't worth much with the sweep after him.
6) b. not to let them hang him in a dress
9) d. sleep in the shed

Page 203
1) b. the priest helping Maddy
4) d. the spyglass
7) b. Thirty years have passed in the story.

2) b. Simon Frick
5) c. Simon Frick
8) c. work on a whaling ship

3) c. He could not leave Tuck behind.
6) c. no one
9) a. the spyglass

Page 204
1) Maddy, Forrest, and Ned
4) Ned
7) Tuck
10) She was not allowed visitors.

2) Hare Heart
5) Face up to your destiny
8) Simon Frick
11) Simon Frick

3) Empty chamber pots and prepare raven food
6) Tower of London
9) Treason
12) the spyglass

Stuart Little

✦ Find Someone Who (pp. 217–222)

Page 217
1) b. New York City
3) d. He felt slimy and dirty.
5) c. The music was quite terrific.
7) c. He didn't know where the hole led to.
9) a. George is easily distracted and leaves things unfinished.
11) b. "Morning Routine"

2) c. Stuart went down the bathtub drain.
4) a. He was working hard rolling ping-pong balls.
6) d. not to reference mice in their conversations
8) d. He pulled a long string attached to the pull-chain of the light.
10) c. a small hammer
12) d. gather small beads on the ground

Cooperative Learning & Literature
Kagan Publishing • (800) 933-2667 • www.KaganOnline.com

~ Literature Answer Key ~

Stuart Little continued

✦ Find Someone Who (pp. 217–222) continued

Page 218

1) b. He got pulled up and wrapped into the window shade.
2) d. placed Stuart's cane and hat near a mousehole
3) d. poured applesauce into the hole
4) a. to respect the dead
5) c. up a doorman's trousers
6) b. a piece of tin foil
7) a. *Wasp*
8) b. The man wanted to beat another boat.
9) c. Mrs. Little thought Stuart might have lost his way.
10) a. "Stuart Lost and Found"
11) b. Is Stuart able to sail a small boat?
12) d. dictionary

Page 219

1) c. A large crowd formed to watch.
2) b. offered to pay Stuart $5 a week
3) c. The people were pushing each other to see the race.
4) d. stormy weather
5) c. paper bag
6) b. He was too wet and mad.
7) b. Stuart was often hard to find around the house.
8) d. being trapped in the refrigerator
9) a. Stuart shot Snowbell with an arrow.
10) a. The family was extremely kind to Stuart.
11) a. Stuart felt Margalo's head.
12) c. Will Snowbell try to attack Margalo?

Page 220

1) c. anxious and scary
2) c. type of boat
3) b. the Atlantic Ocean
4) b. Margalo carried him back home.
5) b. drop his paperclip ice skates
6) b. Mrs. Little presented her with a cake sprinkled with seeds.
7) a. He was terribly nervous and upset.
8) b. He does not care if someone else eats Margalo.
9) d. She decided to fly north.
10) c. A pigeon left a note for Margalo.
11) c. the narrator
12) a. Stuart is a member of the family, and the bird is a permanent guest.

Page 221

1) a. Stuart refused to eat and lost weight.
2) b. a strand of hair
3) c. Dr. Carey
4) c. to demonstrate the man talking with gauze in his cheek
5) b. It had a real gasoline motor.
6) c. One of his teachers was sick.
7) b. make the learning interesting
8) d. King of the World
9) a. Never forget your summertimes.
10) a. Margalo might have a husband somewhere.
11) c. Never push a button on an automobile unless you know what you are doing.
12) b. change into a suit

Page 222

1) a. Harriet was born into a well-known family.
2) c. A girl about two-inches high entered the room.
3) b. to ask her to go for a paddle in a canoe
4) c. a canoe and paddle
5) c. carried it over his head
6) b. He discovered he had been swindled.
7) c. to drink the milk
8) b. It was a mess after some big boys had played with it.
9) d. continued his journey north
10) d. fantasy
11) b. Is Stuart Little able to talk to humans?
12) c. look up information on the Internet

~ Literature Answer Key ~

Stuart Little continued

✦ Fan-N-Pick/Showdown (pp. 223–224)

1) to retrieve his mother's ring
2) Snowbell placed a hat and cane by the hole.
3) a paper bag
4) shot him with an arrow through the ear
5) Margalo came and carried him home.
6) It had a gasoline engine and could be invisible.
7) He was a substitute teacher for the school.
8) The canoe was damaged because someone played with it and it started to rain.
9) He continued north looking for Margalo.
11) He jumped on the shade and got wrapped up into it.
10) He lifted the hammers after they got stuck.
12) He got bronchitis.
13) a man's trouser legs
14) upset and refused to eat
15) north
16) 4 clothespins and a cigarette box

The Whipping Boy

✦ RallyCoach/Sage-N-Scribe (pp. 233–235)

Page 233
Left Side
1) b. tied the guests' wigs to their chairs
2) d. He would have someone else write his name for him.
3) b. He planned to run away.
4) c. The horse was wearing the King's crest.
5) c. a golden crown

Right Side
1) c. The whipping boy shall get twenty whacks.
2) a. to read, write, and do sums
3) c. The fog made it difficult to see.
4) a. bread and herring
5) c. write a letter to the King demanding 55 pounds of gold

Page 234
Left Side
1) b. make fools of
2) d. angry
3) a. Jemmy's whipping boy could take it.
4) c. The King would know the Prince did not write the message.
5) b. the hollow of a dead tree

Right Side
1) c. Jemmy was able to write.
2) d. reread the letter backwards, word for word
3) a. find the nearest rock, sit on it, then refuse to move
4) d. a bear
5) c. Their clothes were torn and dirty.

Page 235
Left Side
1) b. gathering driftwood to sell as firewood
2) c. He wanted to watch for road hazards.
3) b. He had never been allowed to carry anything before.
4) c. Jemmy was charged with selling the Prince to gypsies.

Right Side
1) a. set his jaws and did not let a sound escape
2) c. A bear poked his head out of the coach.
3) a. shaking hands with a prince
4) b. They were sent to Convict Island.

✦ Find Someone Who (p. 236)

1) use it to catch rats
2) It was illegal to hit a prince.
3) read it backwards, word by word
4) Potato Man/Captain Nips
5) The Prince wanted to run away.
6) They were sent to Convict Island.
7) Jemmy could write but the Prince couldn't.
8) Shook the Prince's hand
9) Petunia

Cooperative Learning & Literature
Kagan Publishing • (800) 933-2667 • www.KaganOnline.com